Akihisa HIRATA

Akihisa HIRATA Discovering New

First published in Japan on May 23, 2018
Second published on September 10th, 2019

Author: Akihisa Hirata

Publisher: Takeshi Ito
TOTO Publishing (TOTO LTD.)
TOTO Nogizaka Bldg., 2F
1-24-3 Minami-Aoyama, Minato-ku, Tokyo 107-0062, Japan
[Sales] Telephone: +81-3-3402-7138 Facsimile: +81-3-3402-7187
[Editorial] Telephone: +81-3-3497-1010
URL: https://jp.toto.com/publishing

Designer: Hiromi Fujita

Printer: Dai Nippon Printing Co., Ltd.

Except as permitted under copyright law, this book may not be reproduced, in whole or in
part, in any form or by any means, including photocopying, scanning, digitizing, or
otherwise, without prior permission. Scanning or digitizing this book through a third party,
even for personal or home use, is also strictly prohibited.
The list price is indicated on the cover.

ISBN978-4-88706-373-0

Akihisa HIRATA

Discovering New

Contents

Foreword	008
Discovering New Form	011
Taipei Complex	028
Foam Form	040
Coil	046
Kamaishi Project	054
Gallery S	064
Architecture Farm	072
Tree-ness House	080
Discovering New Nature	097
Alp	112
House of House	124
One-roof Apartment	130
Higashi-Totsuka Church	138
House H	146
Masuya	150
Bloomberg Pavilion	158
Photosynthesis	168
Long House	174
9hours Project	182
Discovering New Commitment	195
Taipei Roofs	212
Museum Forest of "Hill Valley"	220
Overlap House	228
Sarugaku	240
Art Museum & Library, Ota	248
Itukushima Roof	268
Afterword: Toward the Intelligence of the Jungle	272
Project Data	274
Biography	278
Credits / Staff List	279

目次

まえがき 009

Discovering New Form 011

    Taipei Complex 028
    Foam Form 040
    Coil 046
    釜石市復興プロジェクト 054
    Gallery S 064
    Architecture Farm 072
    Tree-ness House 080

Discovering New Nature 097

    Alp 112
    イエノイエ 124
    One-roof Apartment 130
    東戸塚教会 138
    House H 146
    桝屋本店 150
    Bloomberg Pavilion 158
    Photosynthesis 168
    Long House 174
    9hours Project 182

Discovering New Commitment 195

    富富話合 212
    台南市美術館"丘谷之森" 220
    Overlap House 228
    Sarugaku 240
    太田市美術館・図書館 248
    宮島口客船ターミナル 268

あとがき：ジャングルの知性へ 273

作品データ 274
略歴 278
クレジット・スタッフリスト 279

Discovering New

Foreword

New things are an essential part of life. This is because the act of living is an act of continual change. And vitality dwells in things that are constantly being renewed. Nevertheless, when I say new, I don't mean something that is completely unknown without any connection to the past. I am talking about actualizing things that already exist but are remain hidden. In other words, rather than creating or inventing something from scratch, I want to make architecture by discovering things.
We attempt to find new forms in the tangle of things in the living world, and to architecturalize the soft three-dimensional areas lacking a defined enclosure that I refer to as karamari shiro (tangling tabs). Through this process,
I have come to realize that the living world is a remarkable, wild realm made of up of disparate elements that are entangled in a hierarchical way.
As a result, I believe that I can gradually discover the essence of living through architecture. Even the first fluctuations in the universe can be seen as the dawn of life. And architecture can be seen as a new form of nature that arises when we understand the dichotomy of life and death in terms of gradations.
As an order of life, architecture entangles a wide range of other people while influencing and adding an aesthetic aspect to the making of architecture as a form of individual history. The act of making architecture in itself entangles various people by functioning as a formless karamari shiro. This new commitment leads to the emergence of living architecture. Filled with jagged diversity, this is architecture imbued with a previously unseen wildness.

まえがき

　新しいことは、生命の本質にある何かである。生きていることとは、変化し続けることだからだ。生命力は、常に更新されるものにこそ、宿るだろう。

　とはいえ、ここでいう新しさとは、過去と断絶した完全な見知らなさ、ではない。むしろ、既にそこにあるが、未だ隠されたものを、顕在化させる何かだ。だから私たちは、何もないところから創造したり、発明するというよりは、何かを発見＝discoverすることを通して建築をつくりたいと思う。

　私たちは、「新しいかたち」を、生きている世界のからまり合いのなかに見出そうと試みてきた。〈からまりしろ〉と呼ぶ、明確なエンクロージャーのない、ふわふわとした立体的な領域を建築化すること。そのような過程のなかで、生命の世界は、互いに異質なもの同士が階層的にからまった、優れて野性的なものであることに気付く。

　こうして、次第に「生きている」ということの本質を、建築を通して発見しようと思うようになった。宇宙の最初のゆらぎすら、生きているといえるような地平で。それは生／死の対立をグラデーションで捉えるときに浮かび上がる「新しい自然」としての建築である。

　生きている秩序としての建築は、さまざまな他者を巻き込み、かつまたその出来事を〈履歴〉として刻んだ、まだらな美学とともにあるだろう。建築をつくる出来事そのものが、かたちのない〈からまりしろ〉として、さまざまな人びとを巻き込む。このような「新しいコミットメント」によって現れる、生きている建築。それはギザギザとした多様性に満ちた、かつてなく野性的な建築になるだろう。

Discovering New Form

Side

Butterflies flit from one flower to the next. They constantly toy with us and fly out of view as we try to make sense of their trajectory, an almost unfathomable collection of pitches and bounds. Yet, there is a definite pattern and rhythm to their movements. In their own unique way, butterflies understand the complex knot of gaps woven out of the flowers and beautifully surmount these conditions.

Referring to these knotty gaps as "spaces" makes them sound overly ambiguous and dynamic. Besides, flowers and trees are not surrounded by any clear spatial territory. With varying degrees of separation, branches, leaves, and flowers are entangled with each other, creating areas with overlapping localities and gradational depth.

Are these places, marked by beautiful, ambiguous gradations, the exclusive domain of butterflies and birds? Surely not. The same type of dynamic areas must also exist in the habitats of other living creatures – whether it is a coral reef, a jungle, a grassy field woven into the side of a slope, the surface of tree trunk, or a crevice in the soil. This must also hold true for the habitats developed by the human race. If so, we should be able to rediscover and architecturalize these soft areas for contemporary people?

Overlapping Side=*Tangle tab*

The strange coinage *tangle tab* basically grew out of my desire to verbalize this soft knot of gaps. Contemporary architecture has a tendency to focus only of those things with a defined form. Beyond clearly enclosed, tangible areas, and the word "space," there must surely lie an ambiguous regionality that demands our understanding. It was this concept that I wanted to put in words.

Yet, although the term "tangle tab" provides us with a greater breadth of understanding, it would be useful to have a word for this slightly narrower concept of locality. Therefore, I would like to refer to this as a "side." Whether a line, a plane or a volume, some type of side or area emerges in a given locality. When multiple side overlap, they produce a soft and intricate tangle tab.

Beyond "Side" in Japanese Architecture

Among the things that the "side" concept helps us to understand are well-known things such as the places that emerge around a column. In Japanese architecture in particular, the concept of this type of place, formed by a locality without defined borders, is a very familiar one. When I hear the word "side," the first thing that springs to mind is a veranda[1]. Although a veranda might have been conceived as a corridor-shaped platform clinging to the side of a building, this edge or horizontal plane (in this case, we are most concerned with the locality formed on the upper surface) functions as a tangle tab, inspiring various human behaviors on the border between inside and outside. Similarly, the roof, or more specifically, the surface of the eaves, creates a side with the same sort of familiarity as regards the locality of the lower

側

花から花へと蝶が飛ぶ。その軌跡は、ほとんど不可思議なくらい揺れ、飛び跳ね、それを捉えようとする眼を翻弄し、逃げ続ける。とはいえ、そこには確実に特定のパターン、リズムのようなものがある。蝶たちは、花々で織りなされる複雑な隙間の錯綜を、彼ら独自のやり方でつかみ、その流れを美しく乗りこなしている。

このふわふわとした隙間の錯綜、それは「空間」というにはあまりにも曖昧で動的なものだろう。それに、花々や木々は、はっきりと空間的領域を囲い取っているわけではない。多様に分岐した枝や葉や花々が互いにもつれ合い、それぞれの近傍性が折り重なった、グラデーショナルな深度をもった領域が発生している。

このような美しく曖昧なグラデーションの場、それは蝶や鳥たちだけが独占する生の領域なのだろうか。そうではないだろう。同様の動的な領域は、他の生物が活動するフィールドにおいてもそれぞれの仕方で存在する。サンゴ礁であろうと、ジャングルであろうと、たわんだ斜面上に織りなされる草原であろうと、樹幹の表層であろうと、土中の隙間であろうと。そして私たち人類が生まれた生のフィールドもまた同様であっただろう。だとしたら、現代の人間たちのために、このふわふわとした領域を新しく発見し、建築化することができないだろうか。

〈側〉の重ね合わせ=〈からまりしろ〉

〈からまりしろ〉という奇妙な造語は、第一義的には、こうしたふわふわした隙間の錯綜を言葉にしたいという思いから生まれた。現代建築はあまりにもはっきりかたちあるものしか、捉えてこなかったのではないか。はっきりとエンクローズされた形ある領域を超えて、つまりは空間という言葉を超えて、捉えなければならない曖昧な領域性があるはずである。その概念を言葉にすること。

とはいえ、〈からまりしろ〉という言葉は、さまざまな広がりをもつことになったがゆえに、もう少しこの近傍性に絞った概念を言語化しておく必要がありそうだ。すなわち、ここでいう近傍性のことを〈側〉と呼ぶことにしよう。線であれ面であれボリュームであれ、何かの〈側〉、つまり近傍にはある領域が発生する。複数の〈側〉の重ね合わせが、ふわふわと錯綜した〈からまりしろ〉をつくるだろう。

日本建築の〈側〉を超えて

〈側〉の概念で捉えることができるもののなかには、たとえば一本の柱の周りの場の発生のように、今までによく知られているものも含まれる。特に日本建築において、そのような明確な境界をもたない近傍性がかたちづくる場の概念は、親しみ深いものだといえる。〈側〉と聞いて直ちに思い浮かぶのは、「縁側」[1]である。縁側は建物の縁にまとわりついた廊下状のプラットフォームだと考えることができるが、この水平面の〈側〉(この場合は特に上側にできる近傍性のことだが)は、内部と外部の境界上に、さまざまな人の振る舞いを引き寄せる〈からまりしろ〉となる。同様に屋根、とりわけ庇の面は、その下側の近傍に同様の親密さをもった〈側〉を発生させるだろう。

しかし、この〈側〉というのは、アジアの建築になじみの深い空間性を現代風に言語化しただけのものではない。私たちは今や、冒頭に書いたような、蝶の羽ばたきのフィールドさえ、〈側〉と〈からまりしろ〉という言葉で、あ

[1] veranda

surface.

However, these "side" are merely a way of expressing the familiar spatiality of Asian architecture in contemporary terms. As I mentioned at the outset, we can more or less come to grips with something like a butterfly flapping its wings through the use of words like "side" and *tangle tab*. By extending the spatiality of Japanese architecture and the type of locality that can be grasped through a plan, we are able to arrive for the first time at an ambiguous area through more dynamic and three-dimensional side and overlapping them.

Architecturalizing Side

In a project called *Taipei Complex* (2015- , p. 028), I created a kind of urban garden using the side of the volume or frame. This work consists of a reinforced-concrete, rigid-frame structure, soil filled with greenery, and a house-shaped pavilion overlapping with each other in a hierarchical manner. In this area, the building at times floats in the air, and at other times, the side of the hill-shaped setback volume and the edges around the wire rods of the rigid structure overlap, causing the flow of soil and the pavilion to become entangled. A similar concept underlies *Overlap House* (2016- , p. 228).

Another example of this can be seen in *Ukiniwa*[2] (2013), a housing complex project in Osaka. By overlapping the volumes of the building, which rises high up in the air, I created various side, both above and below. This led me to design a garden with a host of outdoor aspects in the locality of the internalized building.

Future Cloud[3] (2015-) is a pavilion proposal intended for an art event on the former site of an airfield in Hong Kong. By extending the geodesic dome-like geometry inside the structure, and overlapping a number of translucent spheres made out of wire rods, I created side that recall a cumulonimbus cloud. The metal rods are formal elements in the large, protruding cantilever-shaped structure that faces the sea. They also functions as devices that cause the cloud-like, ambiguous side to overlap.

Not only are side (the origin of the *tangle tab* concept) the conceptual perimeter in the kind of dynamic, ambiguous locality found in a natural environment, they also contain the potential for a wide range of architectural developments.

[2] Ukiniwa (2013)

る程度捉えることができるからである。私たちのよく知っている日本建築の空間性の延長、Planを通して捉えられるような近傍性の延長に、それ以上に動的で立体的な、〈側〉やその重ね合わせによって初めて捉えられる曖昧な領域がある。

〈側〉の建築化

Taipei Complex（2015-, p. 028）は、ボリュームやフレームの〈側〉によって都市的な庭のようなものをつくり出したプロジェクトである。RCのラーメンストラクチャー、緑をはらんだ土、家形のパビリオンを階層構造的に重ね合わせたこの建築は、時に空中に浮かび、時に丘状にセットバックするボリュームの〈側〉と、RCラーメンの線材の周りにできる〈側〉が重なった領域に、土の流れとパビリオンがからまってできている。同様の思考はOverlap House（2016-, p. 228）にも見出すことができる。

あるいはUkiniwa[2]（2013）という大阪に建つ集合住宅のプロジェクトでは、空中高くもち上げられた住居のボリュームの重ね合わせによって、その上下にさまざまな〈側〉を発生させ、内部化された住居の近傍にさまざまな屋外性をもった庭をつくることを考えた。

香港のかつての飛行場跡地に計画されたアートイベントのためのパビリオンの提案Future Cloud[3]（2015-）では、フラードームのようなジオメトリーを内部にも延長させた、線材でできた半透明な球を何個か重ね合わせて入道雲のような〈側〉を発生させている。この線材は、海に向かって大きく張り出したキャンチレバー状のストラクチャーを成立させる要素となっており、同時に雲のような曖昧な〈側〉の重ね合わせを現出させる仕掛けともなっている。

〈側〉という〈からまりしろ〉の原初、自然環境に見られるような動的であいまいな領域性の概念の周りだけでも、さまざまな建築的展開の可能性があるといえるだろう。

[3] Future Cloud（2015-）

Pleats

A section of cabbage tells us something about bending continuous spaces that are folded up in multiple layers and extend to the other side. If our bodies were smaller, we could pass between the leaves.

House H (2004-, p. 146) is a house proposal for a married couple that grew out of this architectural vision. In this house, which might be described as a single bent room, the couple share a space and while sensing each other's presence, an appropriate distance is maintained, bringing them in and out of view. Although the space is contiguous and connected, it does not afford a sweeping view. But this lack of visibility somehow enhances the sense that the residents are simultaneously dwelling in the space.

In addition to cabbage, this folded continuing space recalls a variety of other things the natural world – for example, a forest spread over a slope. The leaves are concentrated in a thick layer at the top of the trees (known as the leaf layer) that receives the most sunlight. Below this is the trunk area, which blocks the sightline. This folded space between the leaf layer and the surface of the ground has the same qualities as a section of cabbage.

Annaka[5] (2003) is a proposal for a community center for a variety of activities located in a bent space that might be referred to as a "topographical side." The columns correspond to tree trunks and the roof to the leaf layer. Topographical pleats formed by a geometry of rectangular platforms and slopes naturally turn into spatial pleats. In both *House H* and *Annaka*[5], these spatial pleats create an uneven break in the sightline, which results in a complex relationship with the pleats.

Pleats: Phenomenal and Literal

To paraphrase the preceding passage, the literal pleats of a bent plane create phenomenal pleats. In this case, phenomenal pleats produce things like gradients and concentration distribution in a place where a variety of relationships are integrated in a connected space without the use of walls or partitions.

Although this produces phenomenal pleats, literal pleats are not necessarily needed. For example, layering the diagonal openings in the interior of *Masuya* (2005-06, p. 150) created some phenomenal pleats.

The concept of phenomenal pleats can be seen in terms of a higher degree of abstraction. As with the *Masuya*, the direct correspondence to form leads to a more abstract interpretation, defining the differences that fill the place in various ways.

However, there seems to be a tacit agreement that phenomenal pleats are conceptually superior to literal pleats. But when you recall Colin Rowe's *Transparency*, it becomes clear

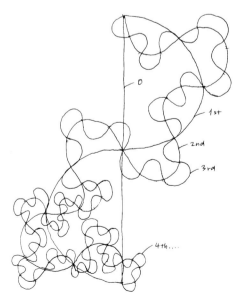

[4] Pleat Principle (2007)

ひだ

キャベツの断面は、その向こう側に広がる、幾重にも折り重なった、たわんだ連続空間の存在を教えてくれる。もし私たちの身体のスケールがもっと縮んで、その葉と葉の間に入ることができたら。

House H (2004-, p. 146) は、そんな建築的想像力から生まれた夫婦ふたりのための住宅の提案である。褶曲したワンルームともいうべきこの住宅の空間では、住人同士がひとつの空間を共有し、お互いの気配を感じながらも、互いの姿は見え隠れするような適切な距離感が担保されている。そこには地続きで連続しているが、一望できない空間がある。見えないことによって、住人同士は、かえってその空間に同時に存在していることを強く感じるだろう。

このようなたわんだ連続空間は、キャベツの断面以外にも自然界にさまざまなかたちで存在している。たとえば斜面沿いに広がる森林を想像してみる。木々の葉が覆い茂るゾーンは太陽光が多く当たる上層部のある厚みの層に（葉層というらしい）集中していて、その下には幹のある視線の抜けるゾーンがある。この葉層と地面の間にはキャベツの断面と同質のたわんだ空間がある。

Annaka[5] (2003) はまさにこの地形の〈側〉ともいうべきたわんだ空間を、さまざまなアクティビティーをはらんだコミュニティースペースにする提案であった。柱は樹幹、屋根は葉層と対応している。複数の矩形のプラットフォームと斜面を組み合わせたジオメトリーによる地形の〈ひだ〉が、そのまま空間の〈ひだ〉になる。House H にせよ Annaka にせよ、そこにおける空間の〈ひだ〉は、一様でない視線の抜けを生み、その結果、複雑な関係性の〈ひだ〉が発生している。

〈ひだ〉——フェノメナルとリテラル

上の話をパラフレーズすると、褶曲した面という文字通りのリテラルな〈ひだ〉は、その〈側〉に、現象としてのフェノメナルな〈ひだ〉を生んでいる。この場合フェノメナルな〈ひだ〉は壁や間仕切りを用いずに、連続した空間の中に、さまざまな関係性を統合する場の勾配、濃度分布のようなものをつくり出しているといえるだろう。

フェノメナルな〈ひだ〉をつくり出すのに、必ずしもリテラルな〈ひだ〉が必要なわけではない。たとえば桝屋本店 (2005-06, p. 150) は、内部に設けられた斜めの開口の重なりによって、フェノメナルな〈ひだ〉をつくり出している。

フェノメナルな〈ひだ〉というのは、さらに抽象度高く考えることができる概念だろう。桝屋本店のように形態との対応が直接的なものから、場のはらむ差異を多様に定義付けるより抽象的な解釈まで。

ところで、フェノメナルとリテラルというと、なぜかフェノメナルの方が高級な概念であるかのような暗黙の了解が漂っている。しかし、コーリン・ロウの「透明性」のことを想起してもわかるように、フェノメナルな透明性という言葉の概念的面白さとは別に、今日においてもなお、リテラルな透明性の周りで動員されるクリエイティビティーが現代建築をドライブさせている。リテラルの生産性も捨てたものではない。

〈ひだ〉の原理

ともかく、〈ひだ〉について考えはじめたからには、まずはそのリテラルな形態的特性や建築的展開の可能性について徹底的に考えてみるのも悪くない。

[5] Annaka (2003)

that aside from the conceptual pleasure afforded by the term "phenomenal transparency," the creativity surrounding literal transparency drives contemporary architecture today more than ever. And it would also be wrong to underestimate literal productivity.

The Pleat Principle

Nevertheless, as we begin to consider pleats, it is worth giving some careful thought to the potential of literal morphological characteristics and architectural development.
As with smoke and certain kinds of marine organisms and plants, there are a significant number of things shaped like three-dimensional pleats in the natural word. Presumably, this is because this form maximizes surface area in a situation where there is a limited volume of air. In the natural world, we can see the need for pleats in action.
I conceived the Pleat Principle[4] (2007) as a way of understanding this type of three-dimensional geometrical structure. Imagine a line segment. After fixing each side, extend the line into the shape of a pleat. This creates a primary pleat like the one between a mountain and valley. Another (secondary) pleat is then formed on top of the primary one. This is followed by a third, a fourth… an endless number of pleats, causing the line segment to extend infinitely. This gave me the idea of wrapping a line segment around a sphere. The first straight line segment is akin to the equator extending around the globe. The primary pleat is a figure that recalls the stitch on a tennis ball. And the highest order of pleats gradually grows more complex while maintaining the basic characteristic of bisecting the sphere. As the hierarchy of pleats deepens, the sphere grows slightly larger, and the trajectory of these line-based pleats turns into a figure that is identical to the three-dimensional pleats found in the natural world.
In *Csh*[6] (2006-08), I applied the pleat principle to a chair. By seeing the pleats as a plant, I made the seat of the chair finer, which ultimately resulted in a distorted shape. This strange plant evolved further in my architecture, as seen in projects like *Gallery S* (2007-, p. 064) and *Architecture Farm* (2007-, p. 072). In these works, the geometry of the pleats functions to maximize the surface area on a site with a limited air volume.

Ecological Niche

At this point, it might be useful to reconsider the term "ecological niche." In ecology, the term is used to refer to the environmental conditions in which a given species lives. But the word "niche" was originally an architecture term, meaning recess or cavity. In other words, you might say that a niche also resembles a pleat.
This diagram showing the geometrical characteristics of an ecological niche[7] is very interesting. It shows that in order to create a more abundant niche for more species, it is better to have more (more diverse) pleats. It might seem like a tautology, but pleats produce abundance in a literal niche.
Yet, the concept of an ecological niche transcends a literal geometrical form. A niche includes both spatially fixed factors, such as the relationship between species regarding food, and dynamic factors. In ecology, a niche for a given species is formed by a tangle of literal geometrical niches and other types of dynamic factors.
This also applies to pleats in architecture. By combining literal pleats with various levels of phenomenal pleats, you can create a rich world. And it is this highly abstract pleat concept that can best be expressed with the word karamari shiro.

煙とかある種の海洋生物や植物のように、自然界には立体的な〈ひだ〉の姿をした存在は少なくない。思うにそれらは、限られた気積の中で表面積を最大化しようとするときに要請されるかたちであり、自然界においてそのような要請がはたらくところで見られる。

〈ひだ〉の原理[4]（2007）はこのような立体の幾何学的原理を捉えようとしたものである。一本の線分がある。この両端を固定してこの線を〈ひだ〉状に長くしていく。ひとつの山と谷をもつ一次の〈ひだ〉ができ、次いでその一次ひだの上にさらに〈ひだ〉ができる（二次ひだ）。こうして三次、四次……と無限の〈ひだ〉ができていき、線分は無限に長くなっていく。この時、この線分を球面上に巻き付けることを考えてみる。最初のまっすぐな線分は、球面に巻き付いた赤道のようなものである。一次のひだはテニスボールの縫目のような図形になる。こうしてさらに高次の〈ひだ〉が、球面を二分割するという性質は変わらないまま次第に複雑に形成されていくだろう。この球面が、〈ひだ〉の階層が深くなるにつれて少しずつ大きくなるとき、この線分〈ひだ〉の軌跡は、自然界に見られる立体的な〈ひだ〉面と同様の図形になる。

Csh[6]（2006-08）は〈ひだ〉の原理を椅子に応用したものである。〈ひだ〉を植物のように捉え、座面の〈ひだ〉が細かくなるように、いびつに成長させた結果である。この奇妙な「植物」が建築に進化したのが、Gallery S（2007-, p. 064）や Architecture Farm（2007-, p. 072）といったプロジェクトである。ここでは〈ひだ〉の幾何学が、限られた敷地の気積の中に、人のための表面積を最大化するはたらきのようなものとして導入されている。

生態学的ニッチ

ここで生態学的ニッチという言葉のことを想起しておいてもいいだろう。生態学で、特定の生物種が棲息する環境のセットを意味するのだが、もともとニッチという言葉は建築用語であり、壁龕（へきがん）、あるいはくぼみのような場所のことである。つまりは〈ひだ〉的なるものだといってもいいだろう。

生態学的ニッチの幾何学的特性を捉えた図式[7]は興味深い。よりたくさんの生物種のためのニッチが豊富な状態をつくるには、〈ひだ〉が多い（多様）であるほうがいいということを意味している。同語反復のようだが、リテラルなニッチの豊富さを〈ひだ〉がつくるわけだ。

しかし生態学的ニッチという概念は、リテラルな幾何学形態以上のことにまで拡張されている。餌をめぐる他の生物種との関係といった、空間的に固定された要因の他の動的な要因まで、ニッチというわけである。生態系において、特定の種のためのニッチは、リテラルな幾何学的ニッチとその他の動要因がからまり合ってできているのだ。

建築における〈ひだ〉についても同様のことがいえるかもしれない。リテラルな〈ひだ〉は、さまざまな水準のフェノメナルな〈ひだ〉とかけ合わさって、豊かな世界をつくり出す。この、抽象度の高い概念としての〈ひだ〉こそ、〈からまりしろ〉という言葉で表現しようとしたものである。

[6] Csh (2006-08)

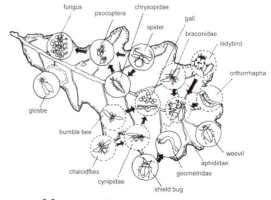

[7] ecological niche

Lines

A procession of ants[8]. The minute path that one ant has walked, the intermittent lines on the ground gradually entangling with the tracks of the other ants and forming a wider line. Faint traces, many small lines overlap and a flow is made. A road as an intertwining of multiple threads, or lines.

When countless water drops overlap, a small flow of water is created. They gradually merge, mingle, and become larger streams. That is why the flow of a river when seen from above forms a tree shape, branching as you go upstream. These dendritic lines form the line of a valley, and various life forms inhabit the valley and its vicinity.

The Japanese word *midori* (green, or greenery) has the same etymological roots as *mizu* (water)[9]. Indeed, plants break down water that is absorbed and drawn from the roots, along branching, gradually finer lines, finally releasing moisture into the air. There are manifestations of the reverse process, which goes together with the river-tree shape as if to form a pair. These are plants. And again, in the vicinity of the plant is a *tangle tab* inhabited by various life forms.

Roads

Many creatures move along the same lines, and when they go over and over the same ground, a natural trail is created. "Deer paths" is one term for these networks of faint lines that peter out and reappear in the woods. The networks stretch their tentacles, expand and evolve like living creatures.

The roads that human beings create are fundamentally no different, and they also writhe organically. Networks of these roads are like tentacles to which cling houses and buildings that humans inhabit. The more various intermittent lines intertwine, the more "fraying" occurs, the stronger this character becomes. Meanwhile, roads such as highways with almost no "fraying" are practically only a means of connecting one destination and another. Biological architecture deals with the former, i.e. intertwining webs of countless intermittent lines. Or,

[8] procession of ants

ライン

アリの行列 [8]。1匹のアリが歩いた痕跡、地面に記された途切れ途切れの〈ライン〉は、次第に別のアリたちの痕跡とからみ合い、太い行列の〈ライン〉をかたちづくる。かすかな痕跡、たくさんの小さな〈ライン〉が重なり合って流れができてゆく。複数の糸のからまり合いとしての道、あるいは〈ライン〉。

無数の水滴の〈ライン〉が重なり合うとき、小さな水の流れが生まれる。それらは次第に合流し、からまり合い、少しずつ大きな流れとなってゆく。川の流れが、上空から見ると上流に向かって枝分かれする樹形をなすのはそのためだ。この樹状の〈ライン〉は谷線を形成し、谷の周りにはさまざまな生物が棲む。

日本語の「みどり」の語源は「みず（みづ）」[9] と同じルーツをもつ。事実、植物たちは根から吸い上げた水を、枝分かれする、次第に細かくなる〈ライン〉に沿って細分化し、ついには空中へ解き放つ存在である。川の樹形と対をなすような、逆回しの過程の痕跡。それが植物なのである。そして植物の周りはやはりさまざまな生物が棲む〈からまりしろ〉なのである。

道

たくさんの獣たちの移動の〈ライン〉、それらが重なり合うとき、獣道が生まれる。かすかで、途切れ途切れの〈ライン〉の集合としての、自然発生的な道。それはまるで生き物のように触手を伸ばし、拡張し、変化する。

人間がつくる道も、根本的にはこれらと変わらない生命的でうごめく存在である。道の周りには家々や建物がからみつき、人びとの生を育む。道が、さまざまな途切れ途切れの〈ライン〉がからみ合う、ほころびの多いものであればあるほど、そのような性質が大きくなる。逆にほころびがほとんどない高速道路のような道は、目的地と目的地をつなぐだけの存在に近付く。生命論的建築が扱う道は前者の、途切れ途切れの、しかし無数の〈ライン〉たちがからみ合った道の方である。というよりむしろ、道というものを有機的な〈ライン〉の一変種として捉えることができるということだ。

たとえば、釜石市復興プロジェクト（2013-, p. 054）では、既存の街を特徴付ける谷筋沿いの道を敷地内にも

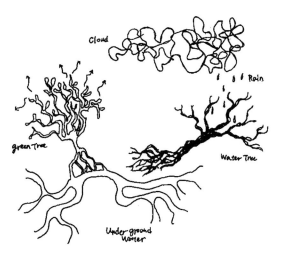

[9] mizu (water)

more accurately, it entails interpreting roads as variants of the lines found in nature.
For example, in *Kamaishi Project* (2013-, p. 054), a road along a valley, which is a characteristic feature of the existing community, is extended to the site, and various human activities unfold in its periphery. In *Long House* (2011-, p. 174), currently in the planning stages, on the coast of Chile overlooking the Pacific Ocean, intertwinement with the terrain takes on a three-dimensional form.

Tangling

When we take lines such as roads into three dimensions, a geometry of folded lengths emerges within a limited volume. As with pleats, many examples can be found in nature. For example, proteins are made up of lines, long chains of myriad amino acids, but folded into energetically stable forms within limited volumes. Ammonites in the special category of "heteromorphic ammonites" form complex helixes with multiple axes within limited volumes, rather than the usual planar spirals. The human intestines may be similar.

In any case, geometries involving some kind of tangling[10] or folding are effective when building lines into *tangle tab*.

In *Prism Liquid*[10] (2010), we sought to create a stereoscopic screen that intertwines with light from a projector, using the geometry of a helix that switches from one axis to another like a heteromorphic ammonite.

Meanwhile, in *Coil* (2010-11, p. 046), a residential building for four families in Tokyo, the living space is an area with passages clinging to the periphery of three thick pillars in the center. This is an architectural realization of lines folded to fit into a small site.

In *Foam Form* (2010-, p. 040), a geometry of tangled lines was applied to the bridge as a network of solid trusses like a skeletal structure. Again, this set of lines is a *tangle tab* for human usage.

Geometries of collapsed lengths are also effective in examining the entanglement of various mobility networks and buildings with limited heights. This approach is realized, albeit in a limited form, in *Art Museum & Library, Ota* (2014-16, p. 248), but more profound applications may be possible.

Here, we have drifted far away from lines as boundaries, and into the realm of lines as *tangle tab*.

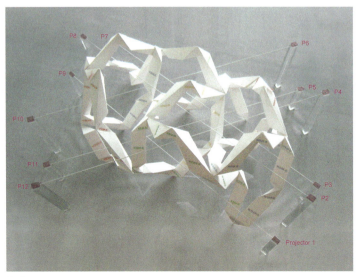

[10] Prism Liquid (2010)

延長し、立体化し、その周りに人びとのさまざまな営みが展開する。太平洋を望むチリの海岸に計画中のLong House (2011-, p. 174) では、地形とからみ合う道のようなものが立体化している。

もつれ

　道のような〈ライン〉の立体化を考えるとき、限られた気積の中に、長さを折りたたむような幾何学が浮上する。〈ひだ〉の時と同様、自然界にはこのような成り立ちの実例がたくさんある。たとえばタンパク質は無数のアミノ酸が数珠つなぎになった〈ライン〉からできているが、限られた体積の中に、エネルギー的に安定したかたちで折りたたまれている。異常巻きアンモナイトと呼ばれる特殊なアンモナイトは、同一平面上の螺旋をつくる代わりに、限られた容積の中で軸が変化する複雑ならせんをもつ。人間の腸も同じようなものかもしれない。

　いずれにしても、ある種のもつれ、あるいは折り畳みをつくり出すような幾何学は、からまりしろとしての〈ライン〉を建築化するときに有効である。

　Prism Liquid (2010) [10] では異常巻きアンモナイトのように複数の軸から軸へと乗り移りながら描かれる螺旋の幾何学を用いて、プロジェクターの光とからまり合う、立体的なスクリーンをつくろうとした。

　あるいは東京に建つCoil (2010-11, p. 046) という家族4人のための住宅では、中央に建てられた3つの太い柱の周りにからみつく道のような場所が、居住スペースとなる。狭小な敷地の中に折り畳まれた〈ライン〉の建築化である。

　Foam Form (2010-, p. 040) では、もつれを形成するような線の幾何学を、骨の中の構造のように、ネットワーク化された立体トラスとして、ブリッジに応用した。ここでも〈ライン〉の集合は、人びとのためのからまりしろとなっている。

　長さを折りたたむような幾何学は、この他にも、登坂力が限定されたさまざまなモビリティーと建物のからみ合いを考える上でも有効だろう。こうした考え方は太田市美術館・図書館 (2014-16, p. 248) で、限定されたかたちで実現されているが、より根本的な応用が可能かもしれない。

　ここでいう〈ライン〉とは、境界線としての〈ライン〉を遠く離れて、〈からまりしろ〉としての〈ライン〉なのである。

Hierarchy

As the world becomes flatter due to globalization, the word "hierarchy" seems to take on luster. In contrast to the hierarchical structures of rigid organization that is the opposite of freedom, we can interpret hierarchical structures as opportunities to introduce depth to a flat world. I had had a vague awareness of this for some time, but the single word "hierarchy" is open to various interpretations. Recently, I glimpsed the potential of what I am calling, for the time being, "wild hierarchical structures," and the outcomes of this approach can be seen in *Tree-ness House* (2009-17, p. 080), *Taipei Complex*, *Art Museum & Library, Ota* and others. Here, to render the meaning of "wild" somewhat more understandable, I will first discuss hierarchical structures in general, which I have examined thus far.

Fractal Hierarchies

The best-known example of a simple hierarchical structure is that of a tree, in which a branching process is repeated at different scales. This is the same dendritic order seen in Darwin's phylogenetic tree of evolution and in the structures governing organizations. These structures in which the same pattern is hierarchically repeated so that the part resembles the whole is known in geometry as fractals.
One of the advantages of fractals in architecture is the ability to reproduce forms using simple geometric rules, in the manner of natural objects. This is not merely a formal pursuit—it is an approach that can maximize the physical *tangle tab*, or niches, depending on its form, and play a mediating role in creating relationships among various activities. Examples can be seen in a series of projects employing our pleat principle.

Proteins

Hierarchical structures exist even in the microscopic world of the building blocks of life. There are almost unlimited varieties of proteins, which consist of delicate hierarchies beginning with primary structures consisting of interlinked amino acids and building up to quaternary structures. In a sense their great diversity, far exceeding that of other combined or multiplied systems classified as hierarchies, makes them extraordinarily efficient structures.
Our installation entitled *Flame Frame*[12] (2009) shows the efficiency of such hierarchical structures in an easily graspable manner. We created the installation by assembling about 1,000 pieces of 100-mm-square pressed aluminum, but the complex structure could not be realized without a hierarchical approach. The primary structures (pressed aluminum units) and secondary structures (consisting of 12 of these primary units each) were fabricated at a factory. Next, we assembled a tertiary structure by combining several secondary structures on site. By adopting a hierarchal process that gradually forms larger units, the complexity of

$$[[[[A/C]/C']/C'']/C'''']/\cdots$$

Fish Poe — Seaweed — Uneven Rock

$C \qquad [A/C] \qquad [[A/C]/C'']$

[11] seaweed diagram

階層

グローバリズムによって世界がどんどんフラットになっていくとき、〈階層〉という言葉は輝いて見えてくる。

自由とは対極にあるような硬直した組織の階層構造とは違い、のっぺりとした世界のそこここに、ある深さが生まれてくるきっかけとして、階層構造を捉えること。

そんな漠然とした意識がずっとあったが、ひと言に〈階層〉といっても、さまざまな捉え方がある。最近は特に、「野性的な階層構造」ととりあえず呼んでいるものに可能性を感じていて、その成果はTree-ness House (2009-17, p. 080) やTaipei Complex、太田市美術館・図書館などに現れている。しかしここで、ことさら「野性的」といっている意味をわかりやすくするためにも、これまで考えてきたもう少し一般的な階層構造についても、整理してみようと思う。

フラクタルな〈階層〉

単純な階層構造でもっともよく知られているのは、枝分かれの原理が階層的に繰り返されるツリーの構造だろう。ダーウィンによる進化の系統樹や統制的な組織構造に見られるような、樹状の秩序である。同じ構造が自己相似的、階層的に繰り返されるこうした構造は、より一般的、幾何学的にはフラクタルとして知られる。

建築におけるフラクタルの利点のひとつは、単純な幾何学的ルールによって、自然物のような形態を再現できる点にある。それは単なるフォルムの追求だけに留まらない。その形態によってフィジカルな〈からまりしろ〉、あるいはニッチを最大化することができ、さまざまなアクティビティーとの関係性を発生させるような、媒介的役割を与えられるからである。たとえば、私たちの〈ひだ〉の原理を用いた一連の試みは、そのようなものだろう。

タンパク質

生体を形成するミクロな世界にも、そのような階層性がある。タンパク質はアミノ酸のからみ合いにはじまる一次構造からはじまって、四次構造に至る精妙な階層性によってつくり出される、ほとんど無限のバリエーションをもつ。同じ〈階層〉に属している事物のかけ合わせとは比べ物にならない多様さが、ある意味で実に効率よくつくり出されるわけだ。

Flame Frame[12] (2009) というインスタレーションでのわれわれの試みは、そのような階層性がもつ効率性をわかりやすく示している。私たちは、約1,000枚の100㎜角のアルミプレス材を組み合わせてインスタレーションをつくったのだが、この複雑な構造は階層的なアイデアなしでは実現できなかっただろう。ここでは、プレス材を一次構造とし、12個のプレス材を組み合わせた二次構造までを工場で作成した。次いで二次構造がいくつか組み合わさった三次構造を現場で設置したのである。次第に大きなまとまりを形成する階層性を導入した結果、現場

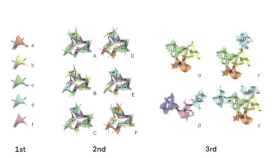

1st　　2nd　　3rd　　4th

[12] Flame Frame (2009)

work on site was dramatically reduced, and a 3D structure with a complexity like a protein could be assembled by artisans without scientific expertise.

Wild Hierarchical Structures

Tree-ness House was the project where we first considered wild hierarchical structures, whose nature differs somewhat from the more geometric hierarchies often noted in the sciences. However, as the term "tree-ness" indicates, we were thinking in terms of fractals and of the transient forms they take on in a wild context. In this case, I interpreted a tree as an ordered system in which different parts (leaves / branches / trunk) are combined in a hierarchical manner, and attempted to construct a similar order with a hierarchical combination of plants / pleats / boxes.

This mode of thinking was later more clearly captured in images like the seaweed diagram[11], as well as with the concept of *tangle tab*. Fish eggs cling to seaweed, and seaweed clings to rocks. Further, rocks on the ocean floor cling to a deeper stratum of the earth… when you think in this way, you glimpse a hierarchical structure like nesting dolls that is in principle infinite. In this context, *Tree-ness House* can be formulated as an architectural realization of this kind of sequential hierarchy.

What matters here is that the elements making up each part of this wild hierarchical structure are foreign to one another. Fish eggs, seaweed, or rocks have different origins, and in a sense are separated by "fault lines." Fundamentally different entities are interlinked precisely because of their differences, and with a strong element of randomness.

I use the term "wild hierarchical structure" to describe this kind of finite relationship among elements, mutually interlinked in a bricolage-like fashion while inherently heterogeneous. It differs both from self-similar (hence homogeneous) hierarchies such as fractals and from the hierarchical phenomenon that Polanyi calls emergence.

In recent projects like *Taipei Complex*, we are more consciously attempting to produce this kind of wild hierarchical nature with the combination of [hut / earth / lattice].

Multiple Layers

At the risk of stating the obvious, hierarchical structures as described above are only one aspect of the natural world. In fact, countless hierarchical structures[13] coexist on multiple levels. However, in practical architectural design, even formulating a limited, specific hierarchy (only three levels in each of the two examples described above) that forms part of this multilayered structure is sufficient to open up innovative architectural territory.

Nonetheless, in principle, it may be possible to capture not only such simple hierarchies but also a somewhat larger part (that is, a deeper hierarchical or multi-layered structure) and apply it to design in the form of architecture, or as part of a city. And computers, with their immense power to calculate, will play an important role in the design of complex manifold structures that exceed the capacity of the human brain.

の煩雑さは飛躍的に圧縮され、一般的な職人の手でタンパク質のような複雑さをもった立体が実現できたわけである。

野性的な階層構造

上記のような、科学の分野でしばしば取り上げられるような階層性とは少しずれた、野性的な階層構造について初めて考えたのはTree-ness Houseにおいてである。しかしTree-nessという言葉からも透けてみえるように、そこでの思考はフラクタル的な発想と、ここでいう野性的なそれとの過渡的形態を示している。ここではTreeを、［葉／枝／幹］という別々の部分が階層的に組み合わされた秩序として捉え、同様の秩序を［植物／ひだ／ボックス］の階層的組み合わせによってつくろうとした。

このような考え方は後に、〈からまりしろ〉の概念とともに、海藻ダイアグラム[11]のような図式のなかでより明確に捉えられるようになった。魚卵が海藻に、海藻が岩にからまる。そしてさらに海底の岩はより深い地層にからまり……と考えると、そこには原理上は無限入れ子をなす階層構造が透けてみえる。してみると、Tree-ness Houseはそのような一連の〈階層〉の、部分を建築化したものだと定式化できることがわかる。

ここで重要なのはこの野性的な階層構造の部分をなす要素同士は、互いに他者であるということだ。魚卵と海藻、あるいは岩は異なる出自をもち、それらの間にはある意味で「断層」がある。異なるもの同士が、まさにそれゆえに、そしてたまたま、からまっている。

このような有限の要素同士が、お互いとの異質性を内包しつつ、ある意味でブリコラージュ的にからまり合うさまを、野性的な階層構造、と呼ぼう。それはフラクタルのように自己相似的な（したがって等質的な）階層性とも、ポランニーが言うような〈創発〉する階層性とも異なるものである。

Taipei Complexのような最近の試みでは、より意識的に、この野性的階層性を［小屋／土／格子］という組み合わせでつくり出そうとしている。

重層

当たり前の話なのではあるが、上記のような階層構造は、自然界の部分に過ぎない。実際にはそのような階層構造が幾重にも重層[13]しているわけである。しかし実際の建築の設計においては、この重層構造の部分である特定の階層構造の、さらにその限定された部分（上記の2例では3階層しかない）を定式化するだけでも、十分新しい建築のありようが見えてくるわけだ。

とはいえ、原理上はそういう単純な階層だけでなく、もう少し大きな部分（つまりはより深い階層構造、もしくは重層構造）を建築、あるいは都市の部分として捉え、設計と結びつけることができるのかもしれない。そしてそのようなひとりの頭脳では同時には扱いきれない複雑な多様体の設計に、コンピューターの計算能力が介在することになるのだろう。

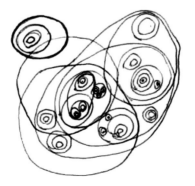

[13] countless hierarchical structures

Taipei Complex

2015–

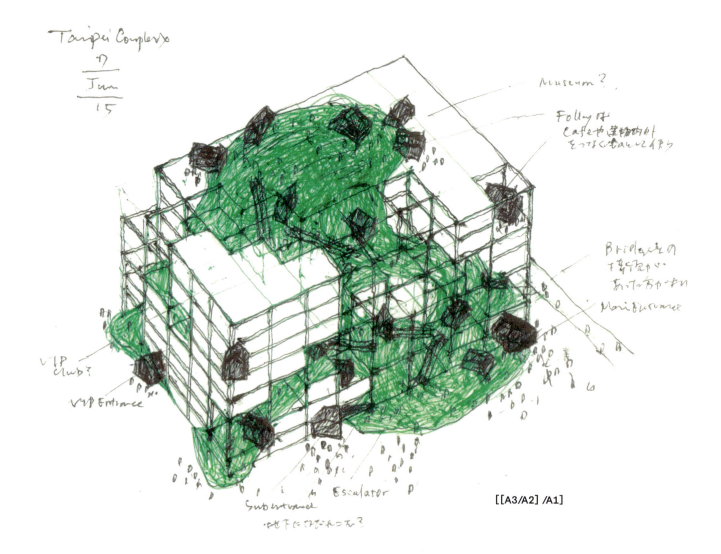

This complex facility was built near Songshan Airport in Taipei. To make a village-like place that would be a contact point in the city, I opted for a layered structure in which disparate systems would become entangled rather than a closed box – or to be more precise, a pavilion with the feel of a village (A3) that consists of a reinforced-concrete, rigid-frame structure (A1) and soil and plants (A2). [(A3/A2)/A1] The rigid frame, highly effective in making a department store-like space, is eroded in places, making it easy for the soil and plants to become entangled. Taiwan, a subtropical climate, teems with robust vegetation. I devised a three-dimensional space made out of soil that would function as a public place for local residents to gather. By simply becoming entangled hierarchically, these commonplace materials (the rigid-frame structure and the soil) gave rise to an architectural framework that was impressive and novel as well as being well-suited to Taiwan. As an additional tangling element, I sampled the traditional Taiwanese form of a glass pavilion and scattered it around the building. This led to a hierarchic symbiosis between these incongruous elements. As a result, the building, the soil, and people's activities are combined in total harmony, creating a scene that could be seen as a village of the future.

台北市の松山空港に近くに建つ複合施設である。閉じた箱をつくるのではなく、街との接点をもつ「集落」のような場所をつくるため、異質なシステムがからまり合う階層構造を導入した。すなわち、RCラーメン構造のフレーム（A1）、土と植物（A2）、集落のようなパビリオン（A3）である。[[A3/A2]/A1] デパート的な空間を効率よくつくるラーメン構造のフレームA1が所どころ侵食され、土と植物A2がからまりやすくしている。台湾は亜熱帯気候で力強い植生に満ちている。台湾の人びとが集う公共の場所としての土でできた立体的な場所を考えた。ラーメン構造と土というきわめて一般的な材料が、階層的にからまるだけで、印象的で目新しく、台湾にふさわしい建築の骨格ができる。ここにさらにからまるものとして、台湾の伝統的なかたちをサンプリングしたガラスパビリオンを、全体に散在させた。互いに違和感のある要素を階層的に共存させる。結果として、建物と土と人びとのアクティビティーが渾然一体に混ざり合う、未来の集落ともいうべき光景が生まれるだろう。

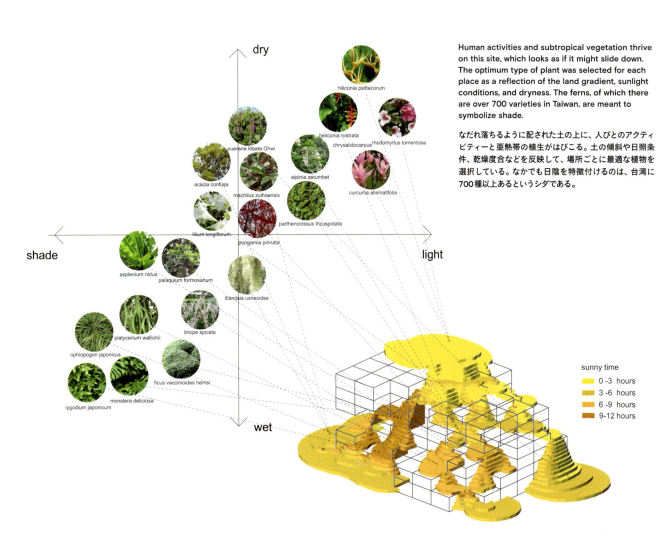

Human activities and subtropical vegetation thrive on this site, which looks as if it might slide down. The optimum type of plant was selected for each place as a reflection of the land gradient, sunlight conditions, and dryness. The ferns, of which there are over 700 varieties in Taiwan, are meant to symbolize shade.

なだれ落ちるように配された土の上に、人びとのアクティビティーと亜熱帯の植生がはびこる。土の傾斜や日照条件、乾燥合度などを反映して、場所ごとに最適な植物を選択している。なかでも日陰を特徴付けるのは、台湾に700種以上あるというシダである。

4F PLAN

8F PLAN

2F PLAN

6F PLAN

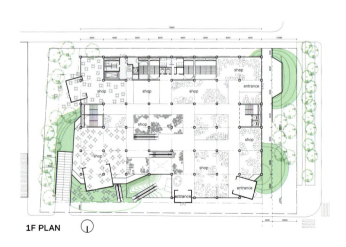

1F PLAN

5F PLAN

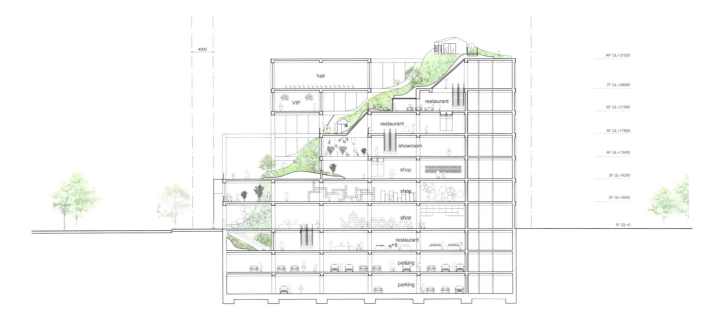

SECTION

SECTION

Entrance
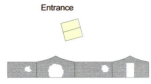

Shop

Restrant
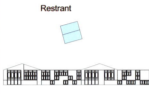

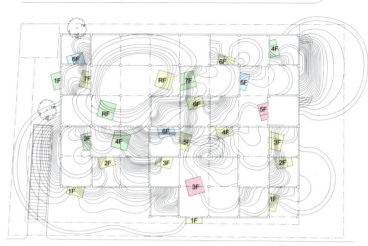

Entrance
Shop
Restrant
Independence

Independence

After sampling a traditional Taiwanese pattern used for the exterior walls of huts, I scattered it across the whole of this glass pavilion. These elements with disparate origins coexist here in a hierarchical way.

台湾の伝統的な小屋の外壁パターンをサンプリングしたガラスパビリオンを、全体に散在させた。互いに異なる出身をもつ要素を階層的に共存させる。

Pavilion study

This is a proposal for a pop music center and an exhibition facility for maritime culture that is scheduled to be built in Kaohsiung, Taiwan. On the vast site, spread out in a U-shape around the mouth of a river, I conceived of a building that would function as a place where the sea meets the land. In other words, the structure would symbolize a meeting between liquid and gas with foam-like properties that were unlike either of these states. Imbued with the genetic characteristics of foam, the structure has the ability to change in response to a variety of programs, including auditorium, maritime exhibit center, small hall, pop music museum, indoor studio, and bridge. It will be positioned around the bay like an archipelago floating in the foamy sea. Made out of a ribbed, steel-plated structure, the building can be manufactured using the processing techniques employed in the numerous shipyards that abut the site. On a conceptual level, a commercial level (i.e., attracting tourists), and an industrial level, the plan takes a fresh approach to Kaohsiung as the gateway to a place that symbolizes the nature of the maritime city.

台湾高雄に建設予定のポップミュージックセンターと海洋文化展示施設の提案である。河口を取り囲むようにコの字形に分布した広大な敷地に対して、海と陸が出合う場所、つまりは液体と気体が出合う場所をシンボライズするものとして、そのどちらでもない泡のような性質をもった建築を考えた。泡の遺伝子をもった構造体は、オーディトリアム、海洋文化展示センター、小ホール、ポップミュージック・ミュージアム、屋内スタジオ、ブリッジといったさまざまなプログラムに対応した変種となり、泡の海の中に浮かぶ群島のように、湾に沿って配置されている。リブ付鉄板構造で構成された構造体は、敷地に隣接した無数の造船所の加工技術によって製作が可能となった。コンセプチュアルなレベルだけでなく、観光客を巻き込んだ商業的レベルにおいても、産業的レベルにおいても、高雄という都市の、海の街としての特性をシンボライズする街のゲートとしての役割を鮮やかに引き受ける提案である。

Installing a water network on the roof not only produced a cooling effect, but also used the downward flow of water to create a kind of microclimate with a combination of micro-low pressure and high pressure.

屋上に水のネットワークを設け、冷却効果だけでなく、流れ落ちる水によって、微小低気圧と高気圧の組合せによる微気候のようなものを発生させる。

2F PLAN

Coil

2010–2011, Tokyo, Japan

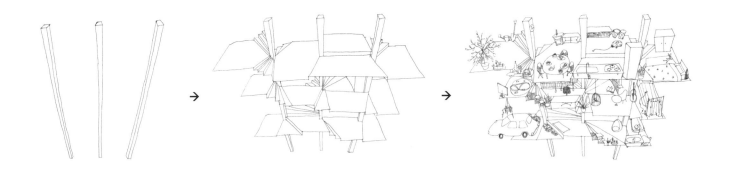

This house, designed for a family of four, was built in a residential section of Tokyo. In designing it, I thought about a new living environment, in which a variety of places would softly connect as they changed. The site was elongated, making it necessary to create a certain number of floors in order to meet the living requirements. This inspired me to make a series of layered spaces with a spiral form that recalls the branches of a tree reaching up into the sky. By erecting three columns on the site, the spiral staircase or floor-like component became entangled with the surrounding area. Then various pieces of furniture and people's lives became tangled together in the architectural framework. And subtle triggers led to other trigger on the next level, creating an even more complex order. In this work, I attempted to make architecture using the type of method that shapes the order of living things. As the spiral was not uniform, but instead changed and developed from one axis to the next, it gave rise to a space with a complex depth. While predicting a use for each space, the expanding spiral determined the degree of restraint and freedom, leading to a vibrant symbiosis between the openness of a natural environment and an organic relationship suitable for a living space.

東京の住宅地に建つ家族4人のための家である。さまざまな場所がふわふわと連続しながら移り変わっていくような、新しい居住環境を考えた。敷地は細長く、生活上の要求に応えるにはある程度の積層が必要であり、そこで、上空に対して枝葉を伸ばす植物と同じような、らせん状の形態によって連続した積層空間を実現した。敷地に3本の柱を建て、周りにらせん状の階段あるいは床のようなものがからみつく。その建築的な骨格の上に、さまざまな家具や人の生活がからみつく……。わずかなきっかけが、次のレベルでのきっかけを生み、より複雑な秩序がつくられていく。これは、生きているものの秩序が形成されるのと同じような方法で建築をつくる試みでもある。らせんが一様ではなく、軸から軸へと乗り移りつつ展開しているために、複雑な奥行きをもった空間が生まれる。らせんの展開は、各場所のしつらえを想定しながら慎重かつ自由に決められ、そこには、自然環境のような開放感と、生活空間にふさわしい有機的な関係性が、生き生きと同居している。

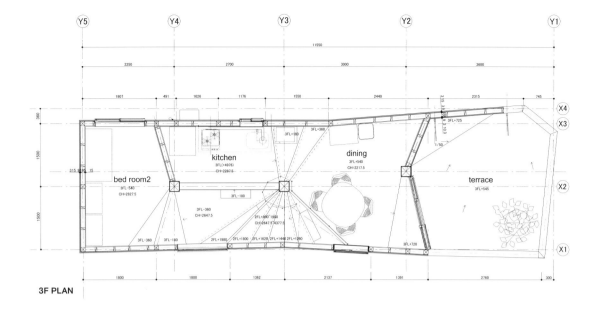

3F PLAN

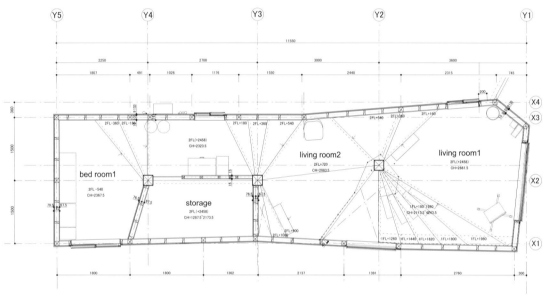

2F PLAN

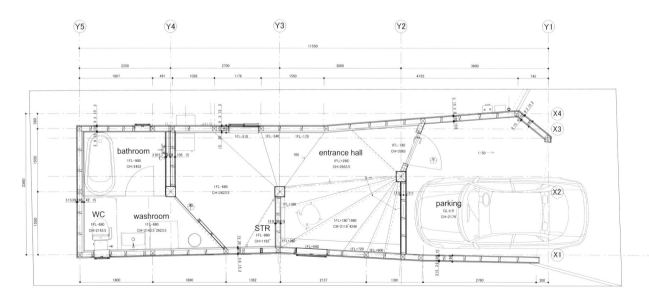

1F PLAN

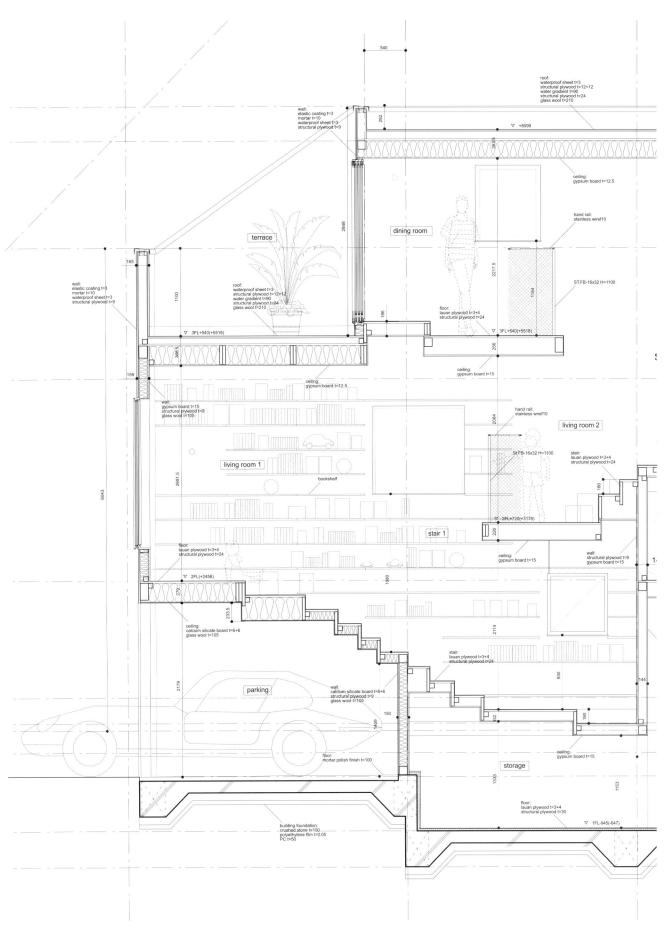

SECTION

Kamaishi Project
釜石市復興プロジェクト

2013-

This is plan for a disaster-recovery housing complex and a children's preschool in Kamaishi, Iwate, an area that was devastated by the tsunami that occurred in the wake of the Great East Japan Earthquake. In this project, I set out to consider how human beings can live in close proximity to nature. First, the city's distinctive terrain provided me with some clues. The nearby roads extended from the trough line and the buildings clung to them. This relationship was also connected to the building site. The road is entangled with the building and the forked road leading to the preschool is linked to the large play area inside the facility. The children play with total abandon in the space, as if they were running through the town, and they also spend time in the classrooms. In the housing complex in particular, I used a branched, three-dimensional design that provides an approach to each unit. The dwellings, which abut the road on the south side and are equipped with a verandah, eaves, and a small garden, are a direct reflection of each distinct atmosphere. The roofs, symbolizing a small common, which neither consists of individual houses nor a single unified volume, overlap to form a continuous landscape. In this project, I set out to create a vibrant, vaguely nostalgic but also very new landscape in which the terrain, the roads, the roofs, the flow of water and wind, and people's activities all became entangled. Unfortunately, due to the severe construction conditions in the area, the disaster recovery housing complex was never built – only the preschool was completed. I pray that the stricken area will be revived as soon as possible.

東日本大震災の津波で大きな被害を受けた、岩手県釜石市に計画された災害復興集合住宅とこども園である。人間がどのように自然に寄り添って生きていくことができるか、プロジェクトを通して考えたいと思った。まず釜石の特徴的な地形が手がかりとなった。周辺の道は地形の谷線沿いに延び、それにまとわりつくように建物がつくられている。こうした関係を敷地建物までつなげる。道は建物にもからまり、こども園に分岐された道は、園内の大きな遊戯スペースにつながる。こどもたちは開放感あふれたこの場所で街の中を駆け抜けるように遊び、時にはそれぞれの教室で過ごす。特に集合住宅部分では立体的に分岐し、各住戸へのアプローチになる。住戸は道に対して南面し、縁側や庇、小さな庭をもち、それぞれの雰囲気が通りに反映される。単独の住戸でも、全体としてのボリュームでもない、小さな共有をシンボライズする屋根たちが、互いに重なり合い、ひとつの連続する風景をつくり出す。地形や道、屋根、水や風の流れ、人びとの営みがからまり合った、生き生きとした、そしてどこか懐かしい、それでいてとても新しい風景が生まれることを意図した。被災地の厳しい施工事情を反映して災害復興住宅は残念ながら実現せず、こども園のみが完成した。被災地の1日も早い復興を願っている。

Kamaishi City Disaster Recovery Public Housing
釜石市復興公営住宅

SITE PLANS

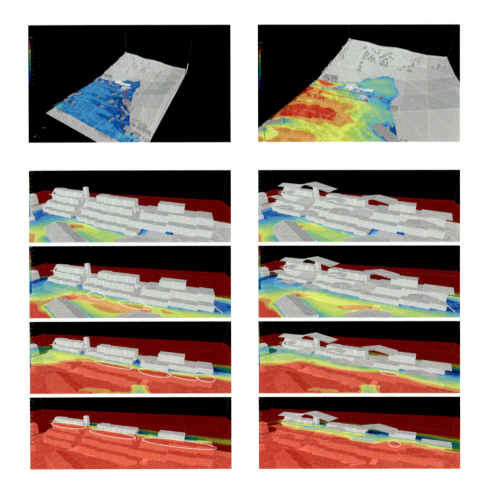

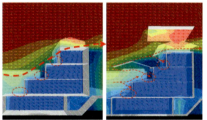

The overlapping roofs introduce the southeast wind, which blows on summer days, into the house and also function as wind catchers, capturing the west wind on summer nights. Without obstructing the flow of seasonal winds to the surrounding area, the roofs protect against the west wind during the winter.

屋根並みは、夏季昼間の南東風を住戸に導くことができ、夏季夜間の西風を捕えるウインド・キャッチャーとしてはたらく。周囲への季節風の流れを阻害せず、冬の西風も防ぐことができる。

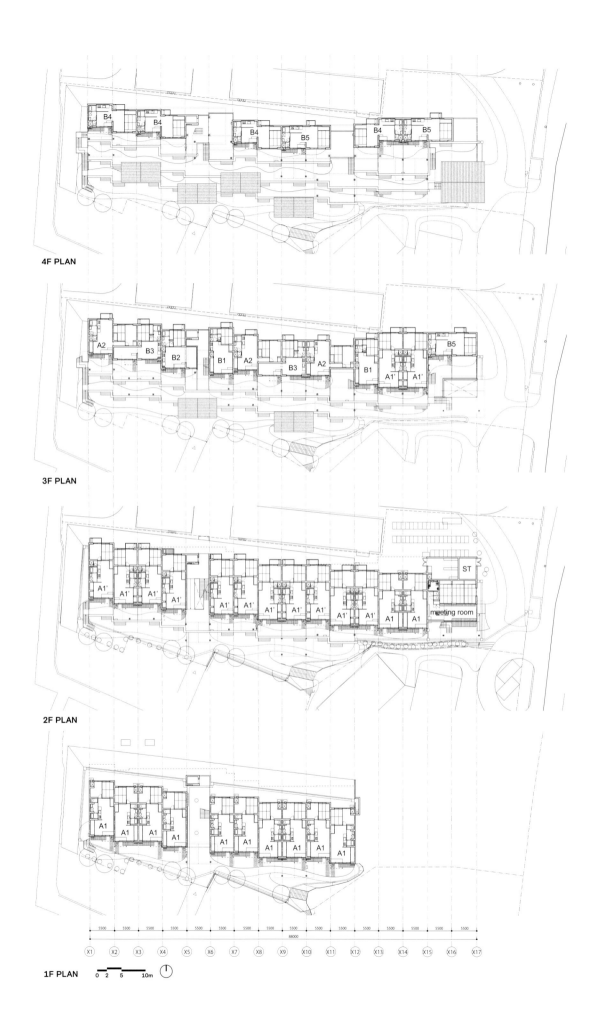

Kamaishi Nursery School
かまいしこども園

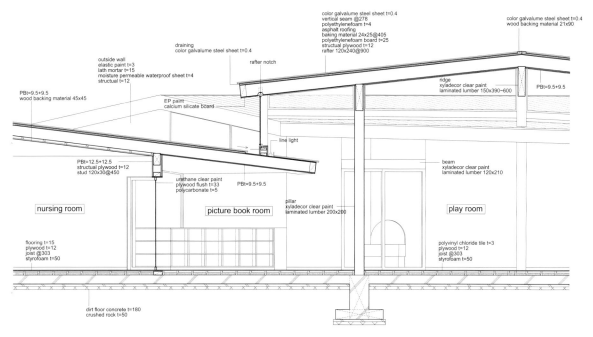

DETAILED SECTION

PLAN

Kamaishi Project

Gallery S

2007-

This complex, which consists of a house, a contemporary art gallery, and a café, was built in Tokyo. In this project for a relatively small lot, I set out to use a new methodology in which the spaces would fold over each other three-dimensionally. This was an attempt to distance myself from the traditional concept of layered architecture in which functions are allocated to each floor and stacked up together.
Smoke, coral, and other kinds of living things indicate the potential of a generative rule for fractals holding that as a hierarchy of pleats deepens it widens. I set out to create an organism-like building in which these geometrical principles could be developed based on external conditions. The space, which could be realized simply through the transformation of a single board, acquired a subtlety akin to a visually impenetrable, continuous space folded into multiple layers. Though the house serves as a vacation home, it seemed that it would be used in a flexible manner – temporarily rented out to an artist for example. It was my hope that the continuous space, based on the pleat principle, would become a lively place in which a variety of functions coalesced.

東京都に建つ住居・現代美術のギャラリー・カフェの複合体である。比較的狭い敷地であり、床ごとに機能を割り振って積み重ねる従来の積層建築的発想から離れ、空間相互が立体的に折り重なるような新しい方法を目指した。煙や、珊瑚などのある種の生物は、広がるにつれてひだの階層を深くしていくフラクタルな生成ルールの可能性を暗示している。そうした幾何学的原理を外在的な諸条件に応じて成長させるようにして、生命体のような建築をつくることを意図した。たった1枚の板がメタモルフォーゼすることによってできる空間は、見通せない連続空間が幾重にも折りたたまれたような精妙さを獲得している。住居はオーナーのセカンドハウス的な役割を担うが、時によってアーティストの一時的な住居として貸し出されるなど、フレキシブルな使われ方が想定された。ひだの原理を用いた連続的な空間によって、異なる機能が交じり合う、生き生きとした場所になることを意図した。

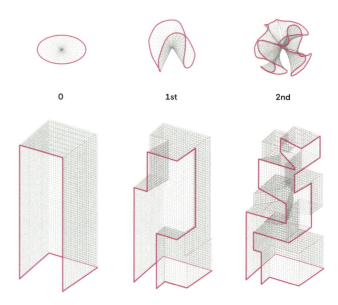

This early plan invoked a principle in which the pleats spontaneously extended outward from the center. In the final plan, however, the pleat principle turned the pleats into genes that "incubated" the edges of the gate.

初期案では内発的な〈ひだ〉の原理をそのまま援用し、広がっていく形態とそこに発生するプログラムとの関係を考えていた。しかし、構造的な負担や周辺条件を考え、最終案では、あらかじめ隣地側の面が壁になる基体としての形が想定され、〈ひだ〉の原理を、〈発酵〉の原理として援用したものになった。

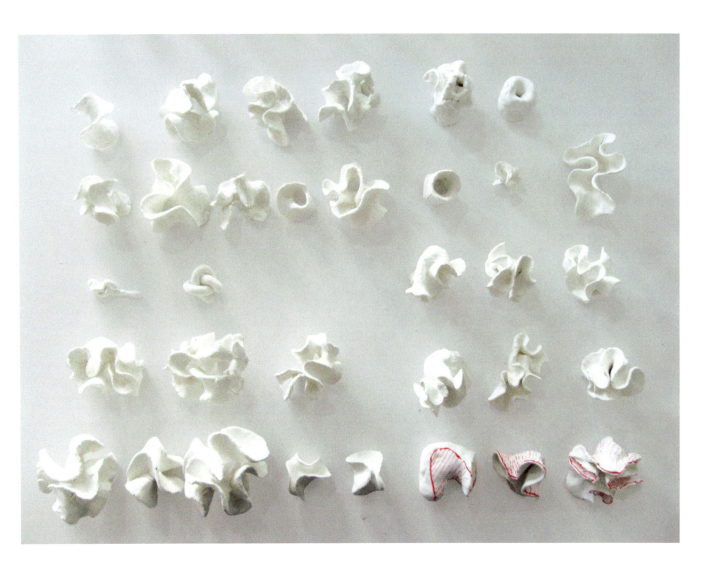

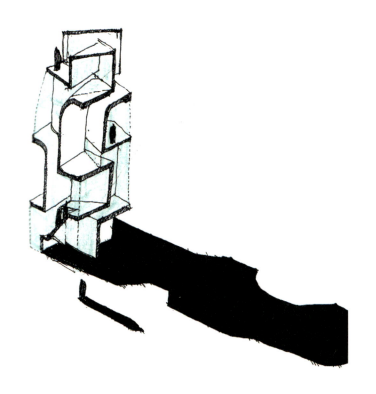

Gallery S

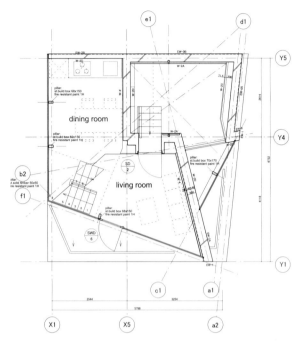

3F PLAN

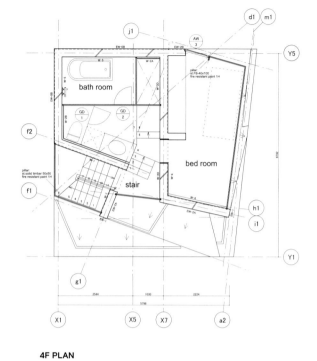

4F PLAN

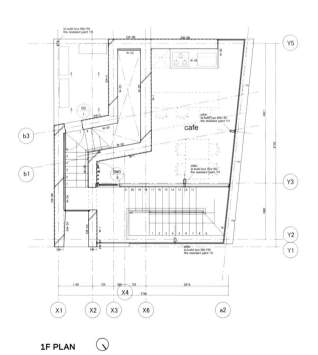

1F PLAN

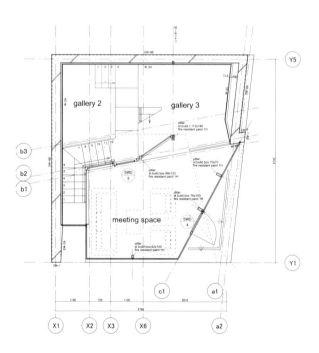

2F PLAN

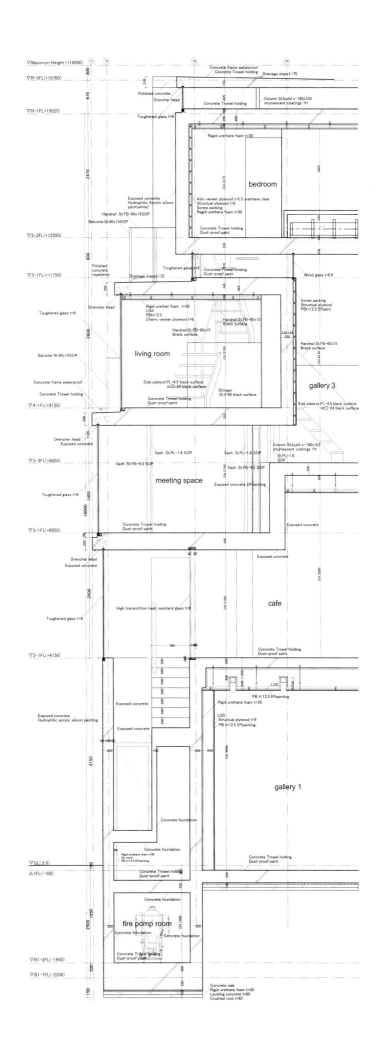

DETAILED SECTION

Architecture Farm

2007–

This is a proposal for a house on a beautiful hill surrounded by nature in northern Taiwan. I devised a surface that could be used to divide the complex program into two parts, the public and the private, and then covered this simple element with pleats. The interior is divided into several parts, allowing the user to turn them into public areas such as a foyer, living room, or family room, or private ones such as a bedroom or a spa. This links the areas while also giving rise to a continuum, encompassing a visually impenetrable and complex distance. Despite the house's complex appearance, everything, based on a fundamental concept, is highly simplified. Using a concrete formwork construction, I adjusted the geometry of the entire building to make 85 percent of the total surface area into a flat surface, and the remaining 15 percent a quadric surface (part of a conical surface). Thus, the spatial landform, made up of pleated surfaces, organically integrates the outside and the inside, and the relationship between various interior spaces, creating a plant-like building.

台湾北部の自然に囲まれた美しい丘に建つ住宅の提案である。複雑なプログラムをパブリックとプライベートに二分するひとつの表面を考え、その後単純な表面をひだ化させる。内包された空間はいくつかの部分に分岐し、パブリックな領域はホワイエやリビング、ファミリールームなどといったものへ、プライベートな領域はいくつかのベッドルームやスパといったものへと自らをかたちづくる。その結果、それぞれの領域は互いにつながっているが見通せない、複雑な距離を内包した連続体を形成する。一見複雑に見えるが、原理的思考によって物事の様相は限りなく単純化されており、コンクリート型枠の施工を考慮し、全表面積のうち85％がフラットな面、15％が二次曲面（円錐面の一部）となるように、全体の幾何学を調整した。このようにして、ひだ状のサーフェスによってできた、空間的地形のようなものが、外部と内部、内部の諸空間の間の関係性を有機的に統合する、植物のような建築である。

When you analyze the program using the pleats principle, it becomes very simple. Public and private is divided by one surface, being subdivided by the pleats.

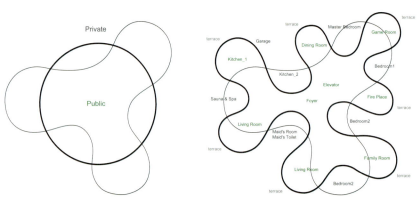

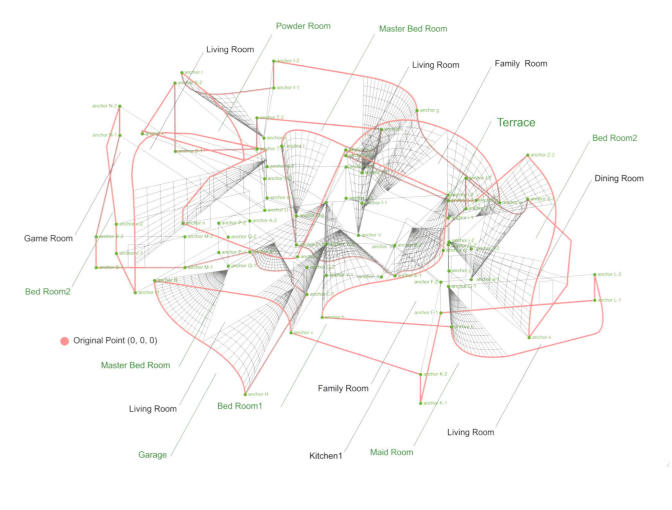

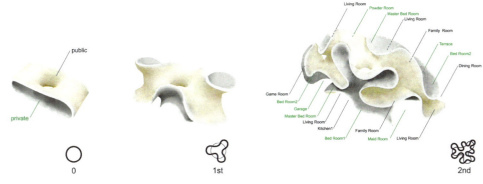

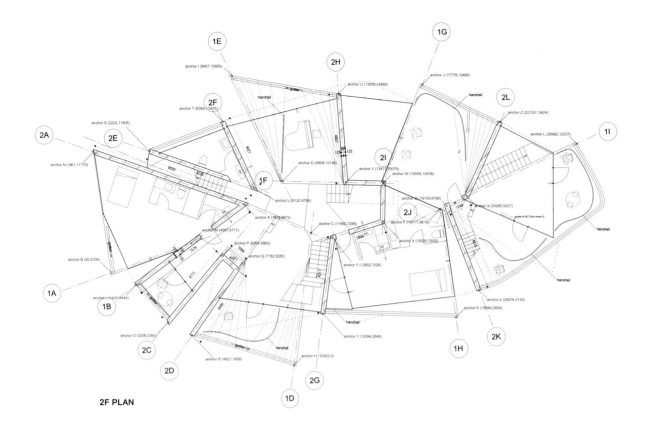

2F PLAN

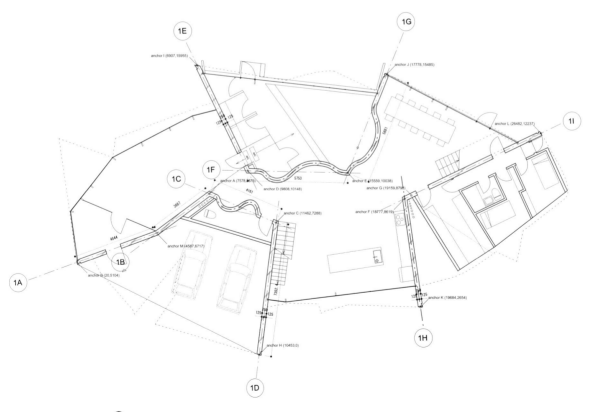

1F PLAN

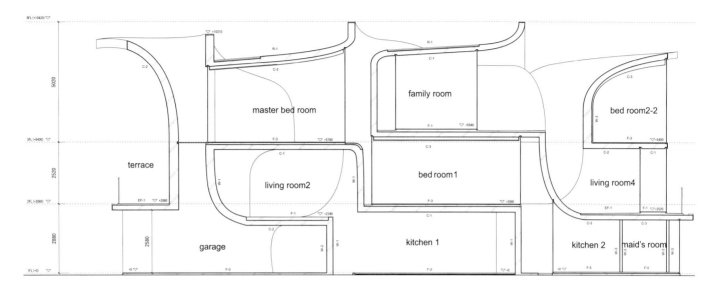

SECTION

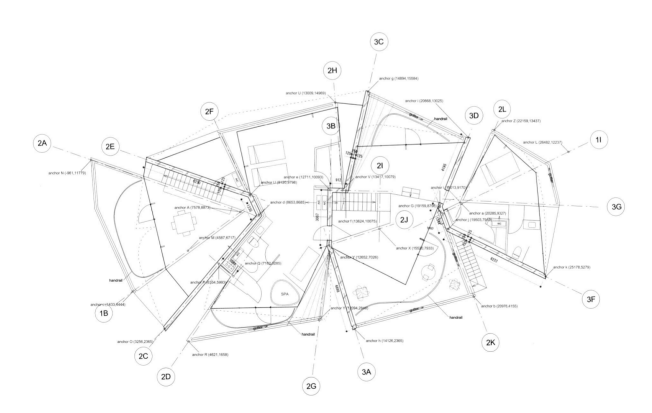

3F PLAN

Tree-ness House

2009-2017, Tokyo, Japan

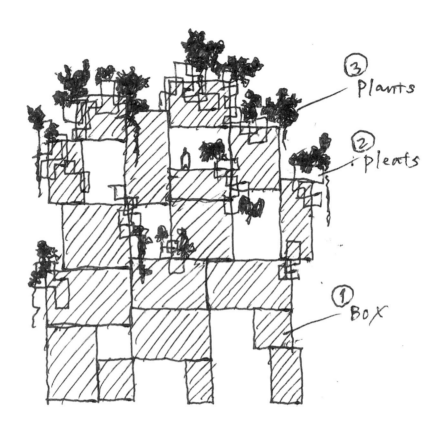

This compound building, made up of a gallery and a house, is located in Otsuka, Tokyo. tree is something that is organically integrated through a combination of parts, each of which possesses different features, such as a trunk, branches, and leaves. With this in mind, I attempted to design a tree-like organic building by combining various parts, such as vegetation, pleated openings, and a reinforced concrete box, into a layered structure. By three-dimensionally stacking up concrete boxes, I created a main structure with a complex void. And the use of pleated windows mixed up the inside and outside while at the same time producing a space that became entangled with people's bodies. Then by adding plants around the pleats, I created an organic whole, which like a tree draws breath from its surroundings. I made relaxed environments, such as a bedroom or gallery, inside the box, and a terrace and garden outside, and created a living and dining room enclosed with glass in several places.Rather than merely making the interior of the building three-dimensional, I made the entire structure, including the garden and the road-like exterior, three-dimensional. I set out to create a house with a futuristic aspect, in which the inside and outside seem to have been repeatedly inverted and mixed together, and at the same time, a wild building that evokes our animal instincts.

東京、大塚に建つ、ギャラリーと住宅の複合ビルである。1本の樹は、幹、枝、葉といった、それぞれが異なる特徴をもった部分の組み合わせで有機的に統合されている。ここでは、樹と同様に、植物／ひだ（状の開口）／RCの箱といった異なる部分の階層構造的な組み合わせによってできる有機的な建築をつくろうとした。コンクリートの箱を立体的に積み、複雑なボイドを内包したメインストラクチャーをつくる。そこにひだ状の窓を開け、内外を撹拌すると同時に人の身体とからみ合うような場所をつくる。さらに、ひだの周りに植栽を設けて、1本の樹のような、周辺環境を呼吸するような 有機的な全体をつくり出す。箱の中は寝室やギャラリーなどの落ち着いた環境を設け、箱の外はテラスや外部の庭となり、所どころガラスで囲ってリビングやダイニングにしている。建物の内部空間だけを立体化するのではなく、庭や道のような外部空間も含めた全体を三次元化している。内外が幾重にも反転して入り混じるような、未来的であると同時に、人間の動物的本能を呼び覚ますような野生的な建築をつくることを意図した。

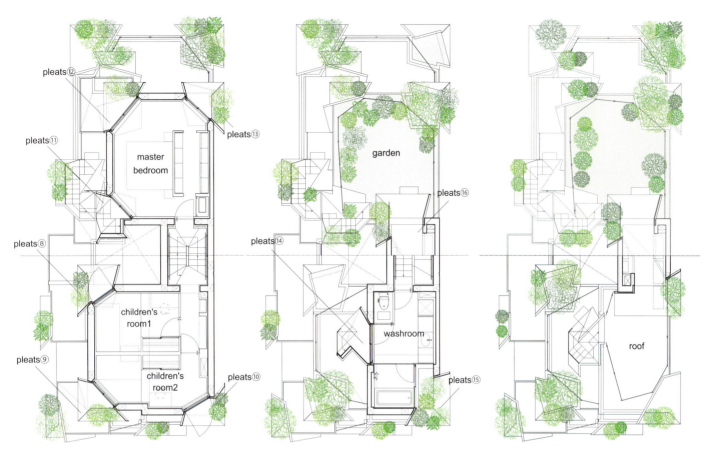

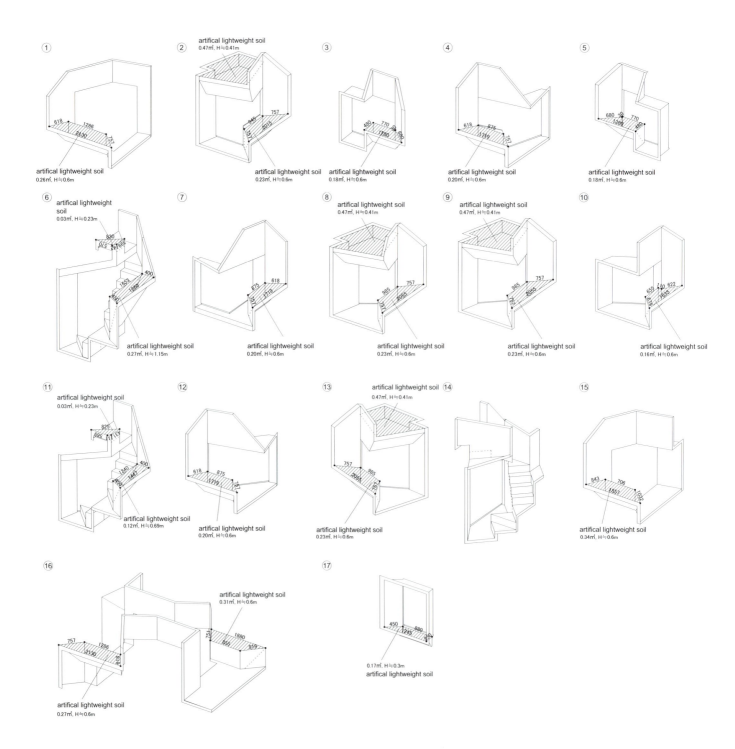

The pleats are made of steel sheets with a thickness of 9mm. After being assembled at the factory, they were transported to the site and installed as they were suspended from a crane. The surface molds were then joined together and concrete was poured inside. (right / Hidden colums and beams inside the box surface)

ひだは9mm厚の鉄板でつくられている。工場で組み立てた後、現場に搬入し、クレーンで吊り上げて設置し、その後、表面に型枠を組みコンクリートを打設している。(右／ボックスにおける柱、梁の関係)

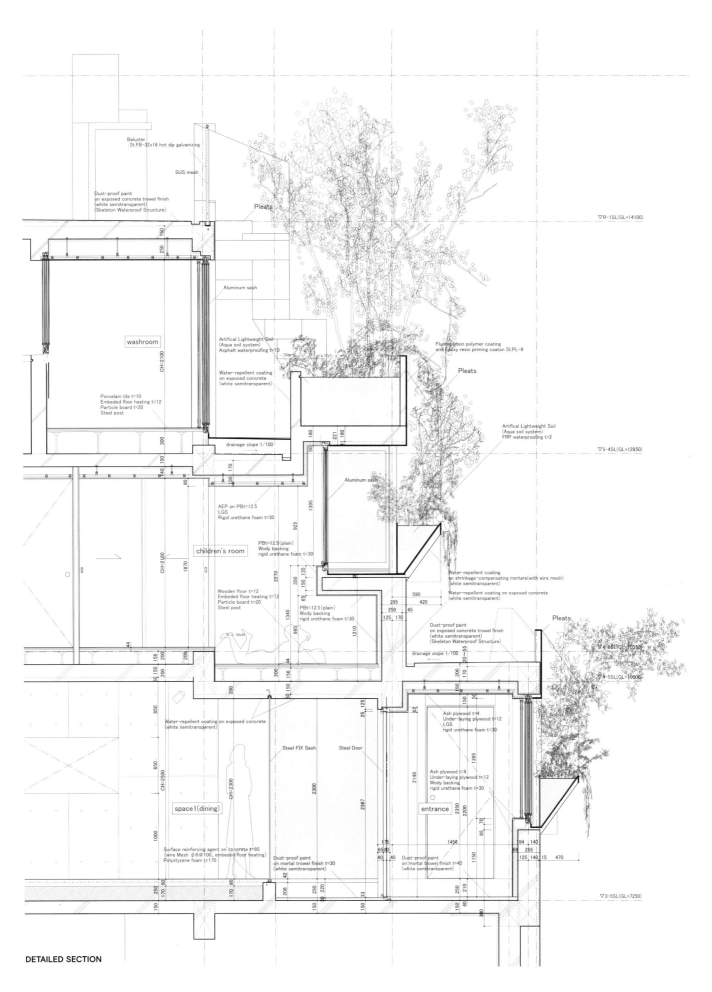

DETAILED SECTION

Tree-ness House

Tree-ness House

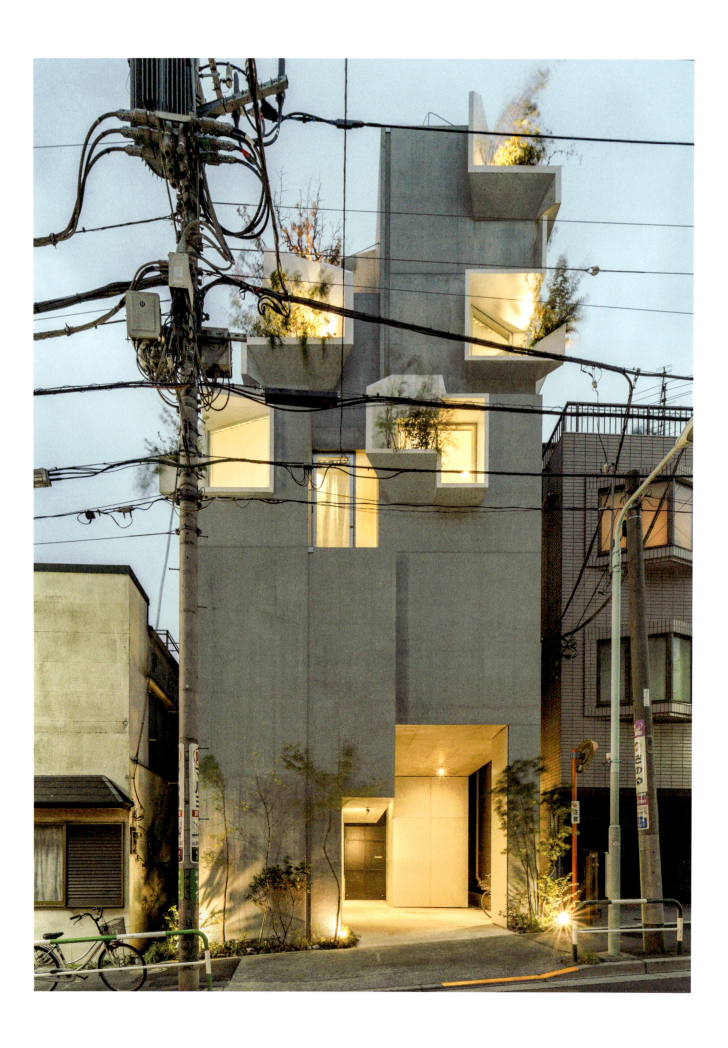

Discovering New Nature

Degrees of Life

The conflict between artificial and nature could be called a false construct.

Roofs as Nature

One example that briefly illustrates this is the similarity between roofs of houses and natural terrain[1][2]. Roofs, which are artificial constructions, and natural topography are surprisingly similar, and this is because the same principle underlies them. A roof is a form constructed to allow rainwater to flow down it, and the natural topography is formed through abrasion by flowing rainwater. In other words, it can be said that roofs are shaped by water. Human beings act as agents of water, if you will, to create a part of the terrain.
If roofs are part of nature, one wants to imagine living under a natural roof, as primitive man lived in natural caves. *House of House* (2006-08, p.124) is a prototype study of such a house. The terrain formed by the roof gently delimits the relationships of life on the roof's reverse side (the inside). The valley line of the roof softly divides the space, while intermittent ridgelines define each individual room. *Alp* (2008-10, p. 112) is an example of applying similar thinking to a concrete housing complex. Here we were conscious of the affinity between roof and terrain.
A more generative approach is also possible, with the roof taken as a body of ridge and valley in motion. It is well known that in natural terrain, networks valleys through which water flows have fractal tree shapes. The competition proposal for an elementary school and *Junior High School* in Nagomicho[3] (2011) is based on reversing this idea so the ridge line forms a tree shape. Here we reinterpreted this complex natural program with a tree of ridge lines. Along the ridge lines were placed seismically resistant "ridge walls," conceiving that these walls would powerfully integrate the whole.

Life vs. Death

Assuming that natural vs. artificial is a false dichotomy, and human activity is always subsumed within nature, it seems valid to say that the true conflict actually lies in nature's bipolarity. It is the conflict between the vibrant nature that we are familiar with and the cold stasis of absolute zero. To give a simple example, the second law of thermodynamics, i.e. the law of increasing entropy, epitomizes nature's implacable coldness. The universe moves irreversibly in the direction of increasing entropy (chaos and disorder), ultimately leading to a state of thermal death, the chaos fading in a whiteout to total death at the end of time. This fate is implicit in the law of nature.
On the other hand, the quantum physicist Erwin Schrödinger expressed life's essence by saying "life feeds on negative entropy." Maintaining order and incorporating negative entropy within a universe destined as a whole for increased entropy: that is the essence of life. This means that in the natural world around us, the one-way journey toward total *death* and the actions of *life* toward gradually building order are two sides of one coin.
Can we treat this naturally inherent death and life as something like poles, and think about it as a gradation of "degrees of life"? In addition to literal (biological) life, the order of the universe can also be positioned within this gradation, as can architecture.
In other words, the axis of conflict that matters is not natural vs. artificial but life vs. death, and the "degrees of life" that we can envision as lying along this axis.

[1] roofs of houses   [2] natural terrain

生の度合

人工と自然の対立は、偽の対立なのではないだろうか。

自然としての屋根

これを端的に示す例のひとつが、屋根と地形[1][2]の類似性である。人工物としての屋根並みと、自然地形は驚くほど似ているが、その理由は両者の背後に同じ原理がはたらいていることである。屋根は雨水を流すためにつくるかたちであり、自然地形は雨水が流れることによって削られてできたかたちだからである。つまり、屋根は水によってつくられている、ともいえるわけである。人びとは、いわば水のエージェントとして地形の一部をつくっていることになる。

ここで、もし屋根が自然の一部であるとしたら、自然の洞窟の中に原初の人が住んだように、自然としての屋根の中に住むことを想像してみたくなる。イエノイエ（2006-08, p. 124）はそのように構想した住宅のプロトタイプ・スタディーである。屋根によってできた地形が、裏側（内側）の生活の関係性を緩やかにつなぎつつ区切る。屋根の谷線が空間を緩やかに仕切る一方、断続的な尾根線がそれぞれの個室を規定する。Alp（2008-10, p. 112）も同様の思考を、コンクリート造の集合住宅に応用した例である。ここではより屋根と地形の類縁性を意識している。

尾根と谷の運動体としての屋根というアイデアで、より生成論的なアプローチも可能である。自然の地形では、水が流れる谷線がフラクタルな樹形をなすことがよく知られている。発想を逆転して尾根線が樹形をなすことを考えたのが、和水町小中学校のコンペ案[3]（2011）である。ここでは尾根線のツリーによって複雑なプログラムを再解釈している。尾根線沿いには耐震性を備えた「尾根壁」を配置し、この壁が全体を力強く統合しつなぐことを構想した。

生／死

自然／人工が偽の対立で、人間の営みは自然の中に常に包摂されるのだとして、真の対立はむしろ、自然の中にある両極的性質にあるのではないだろうか。それは、私たちが慣れ親しんだ生き生きとした自然と、絶対零度ともいえるような冷徹さの間の対立である。自然の冷徹さ、ということでいうと、熱力学第二法則、つまりエントロピー増大則はその端的な例だといえるだろう。世界は、エントロピー（乱雑さ、秩序のない状態）が増大する方向に不可逆的に移行し、極限的には熱的死、つまり乱雑さがホワイトアウトした状態に至る。時間の極限における完全な死。それが自然法則のなかに暗示されているわけだ。

他方で、量子物理学者のシュレーディンガーは、生命の本質を、「生命は負のエントロピーを食べて生きている」と表現した。全体としてはエントロピーが増大し続けることを運命付けられた宇宙のなかで、負のエントロピーを取り入れながら秩序を保ち続ける営み、それこそが生命の本質だというわけである。

これはつまり、私たちを取り囲む自然の中に、完全な「死」へと向かう本性と、少しずつ秩序を形成していく、「生」のはたらきのようなものとが、背中合わせに共存しているということを意味している。
もしこの自然に内在する死と生を、ある種の両極のようなものとして捉え、その間を、生きている度合いのグラデーションとして捉えることができるなら、どうだろうか。文字通りの生命だけでなく、宇宙の秩序も、生のグラデーションのなかに位置付けることができるし、建築もまた同様である。

つまりここで、対立軸として意味があるのは、自然／人工ではなく、生／死の軸であり、そのなかで捉えることのできる〈生の度合〉なのではないだろうか。

[3] Junior High School in Nagomicho

Animalistic

It is difficult to remember my childhood without thinking about insect collecting[4]. Every boy is bug-crazy, but even among them I think that I was a pretty hardcore insect enthusiast. From morning till dusk during summer vacation, I can remember almost nothing but chasing insects in the sun. Anywhere the insects were, from grassy areas to dim forests, to high in the trees, we followed. Such places are usually topographically rich, rugged, with slopes to slide down, and I loved the feeling of being immersed in this environment. It is easier to come by insects when you feel like you have become one. I grew up in a so-called "new town," a massive housing complex in the suburbs of Osaka, not necessarily an abundant natural environment. However, thanks to the old villages, rice paddies and groves of mixed trees irregularly interspersed among the sterile new buildings, there were a fair number of insects. In contrast to these varied external spaces, the buildings of the "new town" were mostly reinforced concrete apartment blocks and schools, and my child's mind perceived the inexpressible difference between the spaces inside the buildings and the natural spaces. I always wondered why the buildings had to be such hard and uncomfortable boxes. This simple thought endured, and became a great motivation for deciding to become an architect: perhaps buildings could be brought closer to the natural environment that insects inhabit.

Human Beings as Animals

Before human beings are "human," we are a species of animal. Modern architecture has been concerned with the human as human, but what of the human as animal? What I am thinking about is the potential for a new architecture that awakens our animalistic instincts. Modern architecture created universal spaces that differ radically from the natural environment, based on clear-cut perceptions, what we call human intelligence. It was a universality that could be shared internationally, beyond national and cultural borders. "Clear-cut perceptions" give rise to linguistic order by segmenting the world using various boundaries and measuring it quantitatively. However, in a natural environment, we act based on "things we vaguely but powerfully recognize" rather than on such clear-cut perceptions. Architecture open to such animalistic recognitions, what Leibniz called *petites perceptions*, has a commonality that goes beyond the international to the biological community, to which we belong as a species of animal, or even to the entire biosphere outside the realm of the human.

Gradation

This differs from the architecture that segments the world and constructs order using boundaries, i.e. from architecture that relies on creating pure, enclosed spaces enclosed within nature and organizing spaces based on differentiation of functions. I envision an

[4] insect collecting

動物的

昆虫採集[4]のことを抜きにして、子どものころのことを思い出すのは難しい。幼いころは誰でもたいてい虫たちに夢中になるものだが、自分はそのなかでもかなりハードコアな昆虫少年だったと思う。夏休みには朝から夕暮れまで、日がな虫たちを追いかけていたことしか、ほとんど覚えていない。目当ての虫たちがいる草むらの中や、薄暗い雑木林のどこにでも入っていった。そういう場所は、たいていは起伏に富んでいて、斜面を滑るように移動しながら、環境に没入する感じがとても好きだった。そうやって虫の気持ちにならなければ、彼らもなかなか姿を現してくれない。幼少期を過ごしたのは、大阪の郊外にあるいわゆるニュータウンで、自然環境といってもそれほど山深いというわけではない。しかしニュータウンの敷地の間にまだらに入り込んだ古くからの集落や田んぼや雑木林があったおかげで、そこそこに虫たちはいた。そんな多様な外部空間と比べて、ニュータウンの建物はほとんどが鉄筋コンクリート造の団地や学校で、建物の中の空間と、自然の空間の言いようもない違いを、幼心に強く感じていた。なぜ建物は、こんなにも固い不自由な箱なんだろう、といつも疑問に思っていたのだ。この素朴な思いは、その後もずっと生き続けて、建築家になることを決意する大きな動機付けとなった。もしかしたら建物は、もっと虫たちのいるような自然の環境に近づくかもしれないと。

動物としての人間

人間は人間である前に動物の一種である。近代の建築は人間としての人間には目を向けていたのかもしれないが、はたして動物としての人間に関心を払ってきただろうか。考えようとしているのは、人間の動物的本能を呼び覚ますような、新しい建築の可能性である。

近代建築は、はっきりとした知覚、いわば人間的な知性をベースに、自然環境とは異なる普遍的な空間をつくった。それは民族や国家を超えて、インターナショナルに共有可能な普遍性だった。「はっきりとした知覚」はさまざまな境界を定めて世界を分節し、量として計測し、言語的に秩序を与える。しかし自然環境の中で行動している時、私たちの知覚を満たしているのはむしろ、「ぼんやりとしか認識していないが強く感じていること」なのではないか。そういう、ライプニッツが微小表象と呼んだような〈動物的〉な知覚に開かれた建築は、インターナショナルという共有性を超えて、ひとつの動物種であるという生物学的共通性、あるいはもしかしたら人間という枠組みを超えて広く生態圏に共有可能な建築になる可能性をもつ。

グラデーション

それは世界を分節し、境界線によって秩序をつくる建築のありよう――自然の中にエンクローズされた純粋な空間をつくることや、分節された機能に基づいた空間の組織をつくることに依拠した建築――とは異なる。はっきりとした境界をもたない世界を、あるグラデーションとして感じることができるような建築が示唆されている。

そのようなグラデーションは、時に地形的な高低差、時に途切れた壁のようなもの、時に〈ライン〉の集合によってつくり出される場の〈ひだ〉である。

360°

はっきりと区切られていない空間では、常にさまざまな事物に360°囲まれていることになる。人間は動く存在であって、数秒前に見たものをぼんやりと覚えているから、このような環境ではあたかも後ろに目が付いているかのように、360°周囲の状況を感じながら過ごしている。それは本を読んだり、壁に掛かった絵画を対象として見たりする知覚力とは異なる、人間の動物的能力である。

人間の動物性を動員することを要求するような建築は、建築史の表舞台で主流をなしてはこなかった。むしろいくつかの建築にその可能性が見出せるような、今後大きく展開するかもしれない伏流として、それはある。

architecture where we experience the world through gradations, without clear boundaries. Such gradations may take the form of topographical elevations, of intermittent walls, or of areas created by groups of lines and pleats.

360 Degrees

In a completely undivided space, we are always surrounded 360° by various things and phenomena. Since humans are mobile animals and vaguely remember what we saw a few seconds ago, in this kind of 360-degree environment we may feel as if we have eyes in the back of our heads. This is an *animalistic* human ability distinct from the perceptive intelligence used to read books or look at paintings on walls.

Architecture that seeks to mobilize the animalistic side of human nature has not taken center stage in architectural history. Rather, it has been an undercurrent evident in certain structures, but one with great potential for expansion in the future.

Michelangelo's entrance room for the Laurentian Library[6] is a rare example of activation of animalistic perception. There is a unique, dynamic equilibrium within a 360-degree space where all manner of things can be perceived. In this environment, people have rich, full-body experiences of their own existence, rather than encountering individual things or phenomena separately and at a distance.

While it differs completely from the architecture of Michelangelo, there is value in animalistically developing the possibilities of interiors with height differentials, known as a Raumplan (German for "spatial plan") as in the Villa Müller[5] by Adolf Loos. This means escaping as far as possible from the constraints of the conventional floor plan with a single homogenous surface.

The above examples of animalistic spaces share the aspect of pursuing 360-degree interiors within limited spaces. However, this issue is open to deepening and expansion, to breaking boundaries between the insides and outsides of buildings.

Animalistic Intelligence

Animalistic architecture is a potential new architecture that emerges when humanistic intelligence is caused to retreat. However, it is not unrelated to the potential of new wisdom that humans are in the process of discovering.

For example, spaces like *House H* (2004-, p. 146) and *Coil* (2010-11, p. 046) gradationally restructure the order of everyday living by not having distinct demarcations. This approach has the potential to define relationships among things coexisting there far more accurately than the linguistically bounded spaces with clear boundary lines between visible and invisible. In other words we see glimpses of a wild mode of perception that interprets the world as a gradation of relationships, a new mode that will evolve further in the Internet era, as opposed to a sharp segmentation of the world. This is because rather than segmenting things, the Internet excessively connects them, and immerses everything in a seething sea of relationships. It may be only our animalistic intelligence that enables us to swim freely in this sea.

[5] Villa Müller

ミケランジェロ・ブオナローティのラウレンツィアーナ図書館前室[6]の空間は、このような動物的知覚を動員される稀有な例である。さまざまな事物が360°広がる知覚のなかで独特の動的な均衡を保って共存している。人はその関係性のなかで、個々の事物と距離を置いて相対するというよりは、それらの存在を全身で感じながら濃密な経験をする。

　ミケランジェロの建築とまったく異なるが、アドルフ・ロースのミュラー邸[5]のような、ラウムプランとして知られる高低差をもった立体的な空間が人間の生活を秩序付ける可能性も、より〈動物的〉に発展させる価値がある。均質な床の上に展開するプランという呪縛からできるだけ遠くに離れること。

　上記のような動物的空間の前例たちは、限られた外形の中で、インテリア的に360°性を追求しているようなところがある。しかし、この問題意識は、建築の内外の境界にも及ぶ、より根本的な展開に開かれている。

動物的知性

　〈動物的〉な建築は、〈人間的〉な知性を後退させることによって浮かび上がる、新しい建築の可能性である。しかしそれは、人間が見つけつつある新しい知の可能性と無関係ではない。

　たとえば、House H（2004-, p. 146）やCoil（2010-11, p. 046）のような空間は、はっきりとした区切りをもたないことによって生活の秩序をグラデーショナルに再編している。このような方法は、[見える／見えない]の境界線がはっきりしている言語的な成り立ちの空間よりはるかに精密に、そこに共存する事物の関係性を定義付ける可能性をもつ。言い換えるなら、そこにははっきりと世界を分節するのとは異なり、関係性のグラデーションとして世界を捉えるような野性的な知のありよう、インターネットの時代に切り拓かれるような新しい知のありようが垣間見える。なぜならインターネットは何かを分節するというよりは過剰に接続し、すべてを関係性の束でできた海のなかに浸すからだ。その海を自由に泳ぐことができるのは、ここでいう〈動物的〉知性だけなのかもしれない。

[6] Laurentian Library

Emergence

The traditional Japanese game *fukuwarai*[7] is an ingenious one. Eyebrows, eyes, nose, and mouth are stuck on a face-shape without looking, a la Pin the Tail on the Donkey. Even if the parts are the same, two faces side by side will have different expressions and will sometimes be so far off base they cannot be called expressions, inviting laughter.

Things like facial expressions, formed by the entire human face, cannot be reduced to individual parts. In *The Tacit Dimension*, Michael Polanyi says of relationships between lower-level elements such as facial parts and higher-level comprehensive systems like the human face: "The upper one relies for its operations on the laws governing the elements of the lower one in themselves, but the operations of it are not explicable by the laws of the lower level." Emergence is the phenomenon occurring in this "upper one" (upper-level system) that cannot be defined by the elements of the "lower one" (level). In the evolution of living things, emergence gives rise to new structures, and the processes of rising up the evolutionary hierarchy are repeated: for example, multicellular organisms emerge through the convergence of unicellular organisms.

In this way, different hierarchies are created and different strata are overlaid. This is not limited to the biological realm. As Polanyi himself described as a "picture of the universe filled with strata of realities," this is a grand narrative encompassing the entire cosmos. A game of *fukuwarai* conceals the secrets of the universe's formation.

Semiosphere

Jesper Hoffmeyer, a leading figure in the field of biosemiotics, advances a similar grand cosmology brimming with life from the standpoint of semiotics, of which Charles Sanders Peirce is regarded as the founder. According to Hoffmeyer, each individual process emerging within the ever more sophisticated order advancing since the universe began is a "semiosis." From this standpoint, communication among human beings, exchange of substances among microorganisms, and mutual influence among heavenly bodies are all equivalent in terms of each one being a "semiosis." Hoffmeyer asserts that semiosis began with a slight "fluctuation" right after the Big Bang. This evidence for this is in cosmic background radiation[8], rays replete with fluctuation that reach us from the outer limits of space. This indicates that at the very beginning the universe was not homogeneous.

After the Big Bang, matter did not expand evenly, the existence of a certain bias triggered the emergence of order in a universe containing diverse galaxies[9], and planets like the Earth were formed. The essential functions of the universe that would go on to produce life were inherent. The processes leading toward life increased in degree as pleats in the order grew deeper, eventually creating life and ecosystems. These are not separate worlds but one endless, continuous one. Hoffmeyer calls this world, in which semiosis has continued since cosmic background radiation began, the "semiosphere." It is a concept that subsumes the entire biosphere of organisms. In the context of the section on "Degrees of Life," the semiosphere is a collective term encompassing not only things that are literally alive, but the

[7] fukuwarai

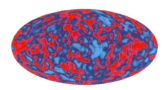

[8] cosmic background radiation

創発的

福笑い[7]はよくできた遊びだ。眉、目、鼻、口。それぞれのパーツは同じでも並べ方で表情はまったく変わるし、時には表情とすら呼べないものになって笑いを誘う。

全体としての人の顔が発する人相のようなものは、それぞれの部分だけをどれだけ注視しても浮かび上がらない。マイケル・ポランニーは『暗黙知の次元』のなかで、この、顔のパーツのような下位レベルの諸要素と、人相のような上位レベルの包括的存在の関係について、「上位レベルは、下位レベルの諸要素をそれ自体として統括している規則に依拠して、機能する。しかし、こうした上位レベルの機能を、下位レベルの規則で説明することはできない」と説明している。

このような、下位に属する要素の次元では捉えられない上位のまとまりが生まれることが、〈創発〉である。生物の進化のなかでは、〈創発〉によって新たなまとまりが生まれ、進化の階層を上る出来事が繰り返されたわけである。たとえば多細胞生物という存在のまとまりが、単細胞の集合から生まれたように。

こうして、幾重にも異なる階層が生まれ、それぞれのレベルの存在が重なり合う。それは、単に生物の世界だけに限定されない。ポランニー自身が「多層的なリアリティーに満たされた宇宙の光景」と表現したように、これは壮大な宇宙論につながる話である。福笑いのなかに、宇宙の成り立ちが隠れている。

記号圏

同じような生命に満ちた壮大な宇宙論を、チャールズ・サンダース・パースを祖とする記号学の立場から論じているのが、生命記号学を唱えるジェスパー・ホフマイヤーである。ホフマイヤーによると、宇宙のはじまりから続く、次第に高度な秩序が生まれる過程の一つひとつが「記号過程」である。

このような視点に立つと、記号過程であるという意味合いにおいては、人間が行っている意識的なコミュニケーションも、微生物が交わす物質の交換も、天体同士の影響関係も、同列に並ぶことになる。彼によると、記号過程のはじまりはビッグバン後のわずかな「ゆらぎ」にまでさかのぼる。この証拠が、「宇宙背景放射」[8]として知られる、かなたから届くゆらぎをはらんだ放射である。それは宇宙のはじまりが等質でなかったことを示している。

ビッグバンの後、すべてが等方向的に拡がらず、ある偏りが存在したことをきっかけにして、さまざまな星雲[9]を含む宇宙の秩序が〈創発〉し、地球のような惑星が生まれることになった。生命を生むことになる宇宙の本質的なはたらきが、そこにはある。生へと向かうはたらきは、秩序の〈ひだ〉が深くなればなるほどその度合いを大きくし、ついには、生命や生態系が生まれることになる。これらはばらばらの世界ではなく連綿と続くひとつの世界なのである。このような、宇宙背景放射にまでさかのぼる、記号過程が連なる世界をホフマイヤーは「記号圏」と呼ぶ。生物によって形成される生命圏を包摂する概念である。記号圏は〈生の度合〉の項で述べたような文脈で

entirety of nature with all its lifelike properties. One could say that the architecture of *tangle tab* is made for the semiosphere.

Organic Iterations

Although the discussion of the semiosphere and lifelike properties is vast in scope, the same processes influence even the smallest things. It may be effective to narrow the discussion a bit and think about the effects of iteration of similar things.
In modern mass production, iteration meant homogeneous repetition and never caused the emergence of an order higher than repetition. In the context of this discussion, it was repetition with a "degree of life" so low it was close to death. In modern times, however, repetition as the greatest common divisor had great significance in terms of rationalization and productivity, enabling production of large quantities of the same things. Today, in the post-mass production era, repetition has lost the importance it once had. However, not every product can become one-of-a-kind or custom made.
For example, living organisms communicate via substances by combining amino acids with limited variation to create proteins with infinite variation, utilizing higher-level morphological features that emerge from amino acid chains. What is important is whether the upper-level order emerges from the iteration of simple parts.
In *Bloomberg Pavilion* (2010-11, p. 158), we made a pavilion in the form of a pleated light receptor using just a simple iteration of a special isosceles triangle, creating what is known as a high plane in mathematics. High planes have the characteristic that when units are laid out in a repeating pattern without gaps, the angles around each point of intersection total 378°, as shown in the figure. This means that the surface bends to the same degree at every joint. Thus through repetition of the same form, like a series of simple operations at a factory, we arrive at a higher order reflecting the principles of pleats and emergence.
While not to the extent of the above example, the same can be said of the *Taipei Roofs* project (2013-18 p. 212). Buildings that can control the deviations of rainwater flowing through the whole were created simply by repeatedly turning square roofs of the same gradient and size in different directions.
Such iterations that subvert the meaning of repetition of simple elements to generate emergent iterations suggest possibilities for the architecture of the future. There is potential for organic iterations that lie between mass production and completely one-of-a-kind production.

[9] galaxies

いえば、「生」の傾向をもつ事物の集合だともいえ、文字通りの生命という垣根を越えて、生命的特性をもつ自然の総体を一括りにする概念である。〈からまりしろ〉の建築は記号圏に向けてつくられる、ということもできるだろう。

生きている反復

　記号圏とか、生命的特性の話は壮大だが、この視点は小さなもののありようにまで影響を及ぼす。ここで、問いを少し狭めて、同種のものの反復がもつ効果について考えてみてもいいだろう。

　近代のマス・プロダクションにおいて、反復とはひたすら均質な反復であって、反復以上の上位の秩序を創発させることはなかった。今の文脈でいえば、「死」に近い（生の度合の低い）反復である。しかし近代において最大公約数的反復が大きな意義をもっていたのは、同じものを大量に生産することによる合理化と生産性であった。これは、マス・プロダクションの時代を終えた今日、当時のような意義をもつことはない。しかし、すべてが一品生産的に、あるいはカスタムメイド的に異なるものになるわけでもないのではないか。

　たとえば生体は、限られたバリエーションのアミノ酸を組み合わせて、無限のバリエーションをもつたんぱく質をつくり出し、アミノ酸の連鎖から〈創発〉する上位の形態的特徴によって、物質を介したコミュニケーションを行っている。重要なのは、単純な部品の反復によって上位の秩序が〈創発〉するかどうかなのである。

　Bloomberg Pavilion (2010-11, p. 158) では、数学でハイプレインとして知られる特殊な二等辺三角形の単純な反復だけで、〈ひだ〉をなす光のレセプターとしてのパビリオンをつくっている。ハイプレインとは、図のように隙間なく敷き詰めたときに各点の周りの角度が378°になる特性をもっている。これは、この面が各所で同じ割合でたわんでいくことを意味している。したがって同じかたちの反復、工場での単純なオペレーションの連続だけで、〈ひだ〉の原理を反映した高次の秩序が〈創発〉する。

　この例ほどではないが富富話合 (2013-18 p. 212) のプロジェクトにおいても、同様のことがいえるだろう。同じ勾配、同じサイズの正方形の屋根を、向きを変えて反復するだけで、全体を流れる雨水の偏りを制御することができるような建築が生まれている。

　このような、単純な要素の反復の持つ意味を反転させるような、〈創発〉する反復はそれだけで、今後の建築のつくられ方を暗示している。大量生産と完全一品生産との間に、生命的な反復の可能性がある。

Fermentation & Erosion

Fermentation

If you look at human activity from the sky with time sped up about a million times, human beings will look like microorganisms that ferment the earth's surface. Along the roads, ridge structures and buildings metabolize one after another like secretions, and colonies, larger in some places, are formed.

For the moment, let us define this slightly odd term fermentation[10] as "anything that transforms some surface into another." For example, agriculture and architecture are altering aspects of the earth's surface in different ways. All of humankind's primary intellectual activities become part of this fermentation process when viewed macroscopically.

Incidentally, the idea of something acting on something else is structured similarly to the idea of *tangle tab*. Or rather, fermentation can be called a state of aggressive entanglement, where things not only cling to substrates but also partially transform them.

Along these lines, I began to consider fermentation in a single building in the relatively early project Gallery S (2007-, p. 064), a gallery and artist-in-residence studio in Tokyo. Initially, I was aiming for a building that acted like a living thing, and utilized the intrinsic pleat principle (p. 017) as is, considering relationships between the expansion of the form and the programs operating within it. However, while such forms are often found under conditions close to those of zero gravity space, when applied unchanged, they create a large structural load. On the other hand, considering the surrounding conditions, it did not seem meaningful to open the building in the two directions where buildings were immediately adjacent. Based on this, the final plan was based on the principle of pleats as one of fermentation, envisioning a substrate where the surfaces on sides adjoining adjacent sites would be walls. In other words, fermentation can be applied even at the level of design of a single building. Fermentation at the macroscopic level is such that each of these individual fermentations interact to create a larger pattern.

Erosion: Architecture amid Flow

In a manner somewhat different from fermentation as described above, aggressive entanglement also occurs when flow erodes a substrate. Consider, for example, when the flow of water erodes the bedrock of a mountain (the substrate in this case) to create a valley. For the moment, we will call this erosion a consequence of entanglement of substrate and flow.

Fermented City

発酵・浸食

発酵

人間の営みを上空から、100万倍くらい時間を短縮して眺めたら、人類は地表面を発酵させる微生物のように見えることだろう。次から次へ分泌物のような道や畝や建物が新陳代謝し、所どころに肥大したコロニーができてゆく。

ここで、この少し奇妙な〈発酵〉[10]という言葉を、さしあたり、「何らかの基体を、別の様態に変質させるはたらき」とでも定義付けておこう。そうすると農耕や建築はまさに、地表面を別の様態に変質させているわけである。人類の代表的な知的営為が、巨視的に見れば発酵作用の一部になる。

ところでこの、何かに何かがはたらく、という考え方は、〈からまりしろ〉の話と同じ構造をもっている。というよりむしろ、〈発酵〉というのは、基体に対して単にからまるだけでなく、基体そのものをも部分的に変質させてしまう、積極的なからまりの様態だといえるだろう。

そう考えると、比較的初期のプロジェクトである Gallery S (2007-, p. 064) で、単体の建築における〈発酵〉について考えはじめていたことになる。これは、東京に建つギャラリーとアーティスト・イン・レジデンスである。当初は、生物のように発生する建築を目指して、内発的な〈ひだ〉の原理 (p. 017) をそのまま援用した、広がっていく形態とそこに発生するプログラムとの関係を考えていた。しかし、無重力空間に近い条件でよく見られるこの形態は、そのままでは構造的な負担が大きい。他方で周辺条件を考えると、隣接建物が迫っている二方向は開口にする意味があまりない。これを踏まえて、最終案は、あらかじめ隣地側の面が壁になるような基体となるかたちを想定した上で、〈ひだ〉の原理を、〈発酵〉の原理として援用したものになった。

つまり〈発酵〉というのは、単体の建築をつくるオペレーションのレベルでも適用できるということである。巨視的なレベルでの発酵作用は、こうした一つひとつの〈発酵〉がからまり合って起こっているわけである。

〈浸食〉——流れのなかの建築

上記のような意味での発酵とは少し異なる、積極的なからまりは、流れが基体を浸食しているときにも起こっている。たとえば水の流れが、基体としての山の岩盤を浸食して谷をつくる時のことを考えればよい。こうした基体と流れのからまり合いをさしあたり、〈浸食〉と呼ぼう。

〈浸食〉は自然の流れが時間をかけて行う現実の過程だが、設計においてこれを取り込もうとするとき、コンピューターを用いたシミュレーションが有効になる。自然の浸食で起こるのは流れが最も抵抗少なく流れるような形態の引き算だが、建築設計におけるシミュレーテッドな〈浸食〉が行き着く先は、もう少し多様であり得る。

チリの太平洋岸に計画されている Long House (2011-, p. 174) では、海から吹く強い風を適切にかわしながら人の活動領域を屋外にも展開するために、形態と風、地形の関係をシミュレーションし、何度かの試行を通してかたちを浮かび上がらせようとしている。この時風の流れ以外にも敷地内外の視線の関係を統合するように、形態を微調整している。こうした過程は、コンピューターのなかでの〈浸食〉過程であると考えることができる。

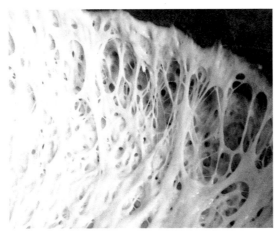

[10] fermentation

Erosion is a real-world process carried out by natural flows over time, but computer simulations are effective for incorporating it into design. What occurs with natural erosion is the subtraction of areas that have the least resistance to flow, but simulated erosion in architectural design can lead in somewhat more diverse directions.

In *Long House* (2011-, p. 174) planned for construction on the Pacific coast of Chile, to expand the scope of human activity outdoors appropriately while taking into account the strong wind blowing from the sea, we simulated the relationships among forms, wind, and terrain, and conducted repeated trials to arrive at a final design. In doing so, we not only took wind into account, but also fine-tuned the form so as to integrate the lines of sight inside and outside the site. This process can be thought of as a process of erosion taking place inside a computer.

As concepts, fermentation and erosion are open to various developments beyond the framework of proliferating geometries and optimization through simulation. For example, in *Kotoriku*[11] (2012-14), an apartment building in Tokyo, walls built following a distorted grid, reflecting the surrounding urban zoning, are eroded like hills. Earth and various plants are inserted into gaps opened by the erosion, creating an area like a three-dimensional garden shared by residents. Or, in the capsule hotel *9hours Asakusa* (2016-18, p. 182) in Asakusa, Tokyo, a substrate like a cliff face made of small-scale capsules is eroded by the ongoing flow from the bustle of small stores in Asakusa. The entanglement of the basic program and the flow of people from the city that erodes it seem to be a product of a single, comprehensive fermentation process.

Ruins

Architecture created through fermentation and erosion somehow resembles ruins. This is because the word "ruins" implies human-made structures just before returning to nature, where artificial order is eroded by natural activity. Human activity and nature's various activities compete with one another. In ruins, this conflict manifests itself after human activity has already ceased. However, is it possible to design buildings that incorporate this mutual antagonism from the beginning? That is one of the questions we are addressing here.

概念としての〈発酵〉とか〈浸食〉は、増殖する幾何学とか、シミュレーションによる最適化、といった枠組みを超えてさまざまな展開に開かれている。たとえば、東京の集合住宅Kotoriku[11]（2012-14）では、周辺の街割りを反映したひずんだグリッドに沿って建ち上がった壁が、丘のように〈浸食〉されている。削られてできた空隙に、土とさまざまな植物が入り込み、住民に共有される立体的な庭のような場所ができている。あるいは、東京浅草に建つカプセルホテル9hours Asakusa（2016-18, p. 182）では、微細なスケールのカプセルからできた岩山のような基体を、浅草の小店舗の賑わいから連続するような道の流れが〈浸食〉している。ベースとなるプログラムとそれを〈浸食〉する街からの人の流れのからまり合いは、全体としてひとつの発酵過程の産物のようにみえる。

廃墟

〈発酵〉や〈浸食〉によってつくられる建築は、どこか廃墟に似るだろう。なぜなら廃墟とは、人工的な秩序が自然の営みによって〈浸食〉され、自然の中に戻る直前の様相を捉えた言葉だからだ。人間の営みと、それとは異なる自然の営みが拮抗し合っている。廃墟においては、人の営みが行われなくなった後で、その拮抗が現れる。しかし、そもそものはじまりから、両者の拮抗をあらかじめ内包したような建築を設計することは可能か。ここでの問いは、そのようなものである。

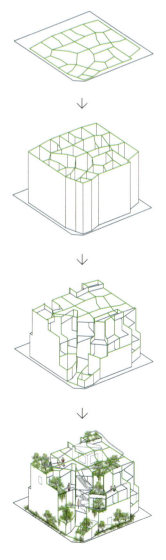

[11] Kotoriku (2012-14)

This housing complex was built in Akabane, Tokyo. The site was located on a plateau, which still retained some mountain folds and looked out over a complex pattern of roofs that recalled a mountain range. On this three-dimensional terrain, I thought it would be better to make a building that would convey the wrinkles created by the elevated ground rather than making a simple boxlike domain. Accepting the natural terrain, which had been shaped by rainwater, I created an undulating roof and walls, and an alley-shaped gap as an approach to the house in the volume. The black concrete exterior, enveloped in this uneven surface, naturally gave form to the interior. Each room reflects the conflict between the interior and the exterior, and when you are inside, you can sense a larger order. The architecture, born of the emergence of a natural landform and a methodology that recalls cell division, made a house that was unexpectedly suited to the landscape, which is characterized by rows of roofs.

東京、赤羽に建つ集合住宅である。敷地は山襞の残る高台にあり、眼下には複雑な形状の屋根が山並みのように連なる。立体的な地形の中で、建築を、単純な箱状の領域でつくるというよりは、地面が隆起してできたしわのようなものとして捉え直せないだろうか。雨水によって生成される自然の地形を引き継ぎ、建築のボリュームに、起伏をもった屋根や壁、住戸へのアプローチとなる路地状の隙間をつくる。こうした凹凸をまとった黒いコンクリートの外観は、そのまま室内に生かされる。それぞれの部屋はこうした内外のせめぎ合いが反映され、室内に居ながらにして、より大きな秩序を感じることができる。自然の地形の生成や、細胞分裂の過程を思わせる方法によって生まれた建築は、思いのほか一戸建ての住居が建ち並ぶ屋根の連なる風景になじんでいる。

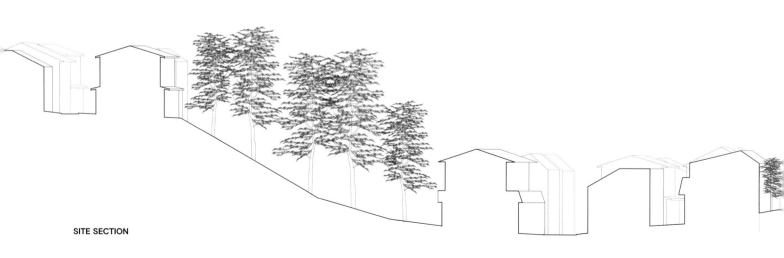

SITE SECTION

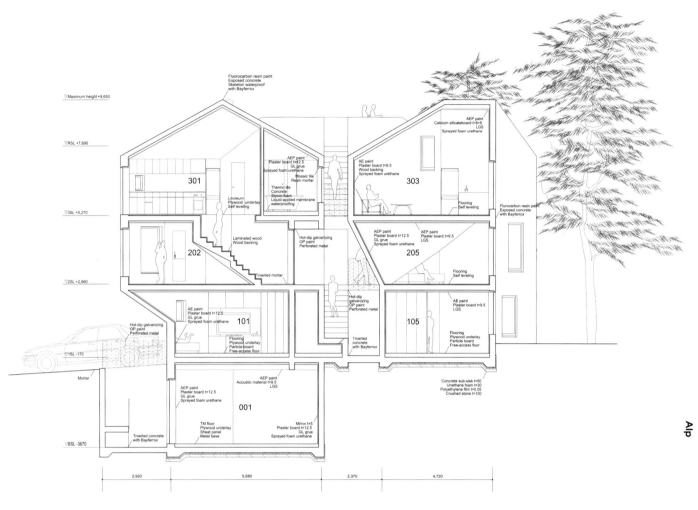

SECTION

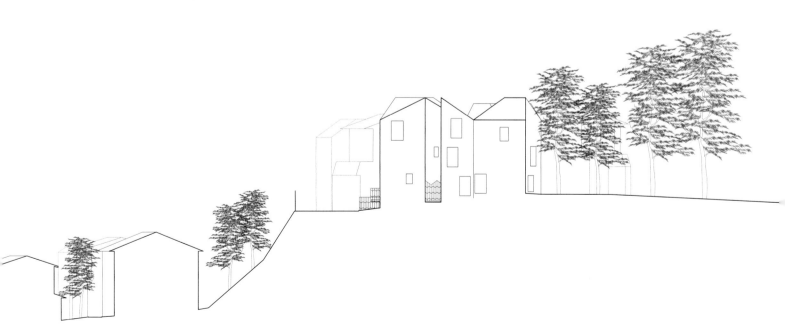

2F PLAN

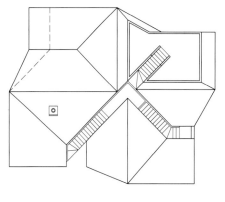

RF PLAN

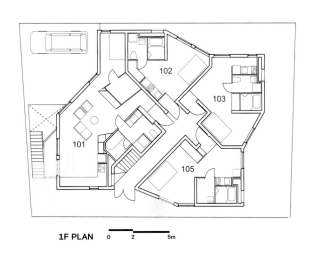

1F PLAN 0 2 5m

3F PLAN

SITE PLAN

House of House
イエノイエ

2006-2008, Kanagawa, Japan

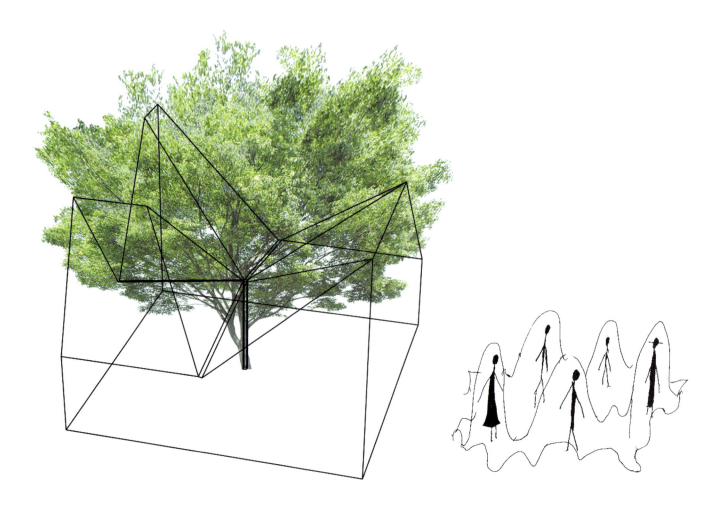

House of House is a residential model that attempts to throw fresh light on the form of the house and roof. When you gaze down at a series of roofs from the sky, they vaguely recall a mountain range. Although a mountain is a form that is created by running water, a roof is a form that is designed to shed water (rain). Behind these formal similarities, we can detect the same underlying principle. Therefore, we might conclude that a roof is a wondrous entity that is closely tied to nature. I imagined how it would be to live inside a place with a natural environment created by a roof. This inspired me to make a plan with a combination of lightly segmented roofs connecting a number of two-story buildings with private rooms. Although the lower floor is closed, the upper one is open. The visually impenetrable, continuous space created by the upper floor, containing a common space and private rooms, simultaneously gives rise to a sense of unity and a sense of comfort among the people who co-inhabit the building. This proposal for a new residential space combines a sense of security based on returning to a primitive dwelling, with a sense of awe in regard to the roof.

イエノイエは、家型あるいは屋根というものに新しい解釈を与えることを試みた住宅のモデルである。屋根の連なりを上空から眺めると、どこか山脈に似ている。山脈は水が流れることによってできるかたちであるのに対し、屋根は（雨）水を流すためにつくるかたちだからだ。似たかたちの背後に同じ原理を見出すことができる。この意味で、屋根はきわめて自然に近い不思議な存在であるということができる。この屋根のつくり出す自然環境のような場所にダイレクトに住まうことをイメージした。そこで、複数の２階建ての個室とその間をやわらかく分節する屋根の組み合わせを提案する。個室の下層はクローズドな場所で、上層はオープンな場所である。共用空間と個室の上層がかたちづくる見通せない連続空間は、複数の人がともに住む一体感と互いの心地良い距離感を同時につくり出す。イエノイエは原初の住居に戻るような懐かしさと、屋根という存在に出合う驚きを合わせもつ、新しい居住空間の提案である。

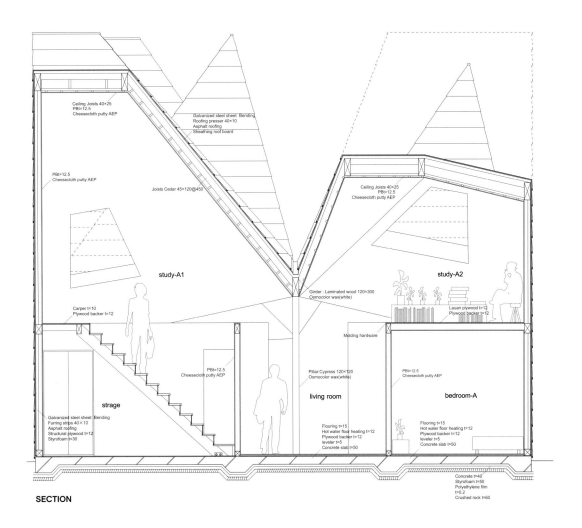
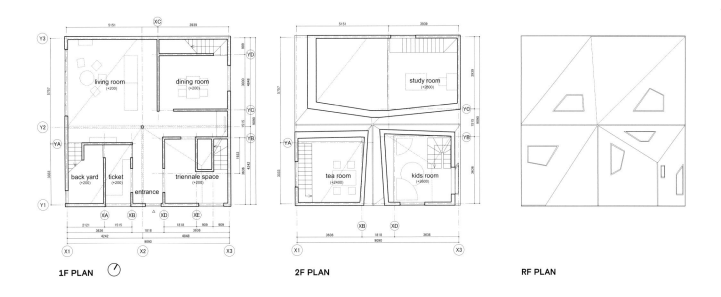

One-roof Apartment

2007-2010, Niigata, Japan

SOUTH ELEVATION

This housing complex is located in Joetsu, Niigata. For this project, I decided to create a public space covered with a roof formed by the building's volume. This recalled the large roofs of folk dwellings in the region, which is known for its heavy snowfalls. When you divide the entire (presumably square) volume, you end up with spaces in between. A warm and benevolent air volume, offering protection from the cold of the outside world, welcomes the resident inside. The unique appearance of the branched volume functions as a contemporary symbol for this type of warm place. Here, people live in a space that seems to exist inside a roof. Meanwhile, the common space beneath it serves as a present-day *doma* (earthen floor). There are two types of houses, a single-story dwelling and a maisonette, both of which have windows facing the mountains on the south side. These wondrous roof-like houses, located in the midst of a robust natural setting, have a contemporary air but are designed for a slightly nostalgic way of living.

新潟、上越市に建つ集合住宅である。ここでは雪国の民家の大屋根よろしく、住戸のボリュームでできた屋根状の覆いで共用のスペースをつくり出すことを考えた。通常想定される四角い全体ボリュームをふたつに分岐させると、その間にスペースができる。寒い屋外から囲い取られた暖かくておおらかな気積が、住人を迎え入れる。枝分かれしたボリュームがつくる独特の外観は、そういう暖かな場所を現代的にシンボライズするだろう。ここで人が住むのは屋根の中のような場所であり、その下の共用のスペースは現代の「土間」である。住戸はフラットタイプとメゾネットタイプの2種類あり、それぞれ南側の山並みに開かれた窓をもつ。骨太な自然の中に建つ、屋根の中のような不思議な家が、現代的だがどこか懐かしい暮らしのための場所となるだろう。

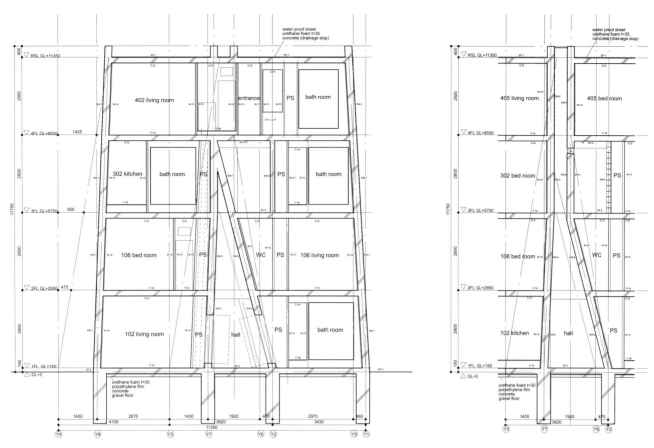

SECTION

One-roof Apartment

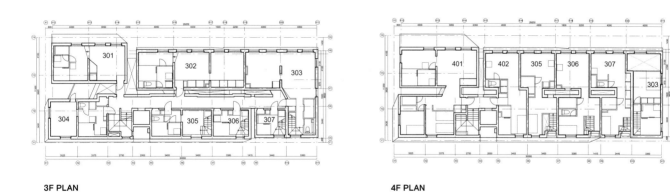

3F PLAN

4F PLAN

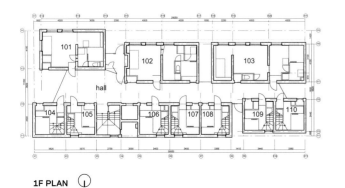

1F PLAN

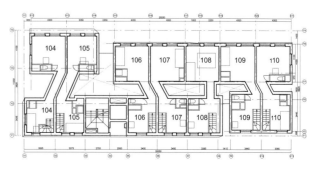

2F PLAN

One-roof Apartment

135

Higashi-Totsuka Church
東戸塚教会

2012–2015, Kanagawa, Japan

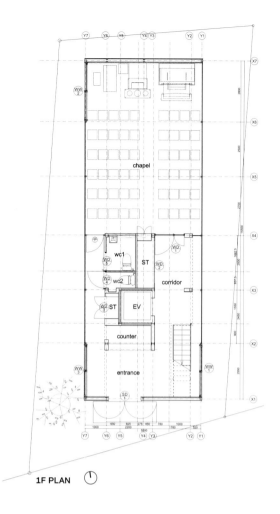

1F PLAN

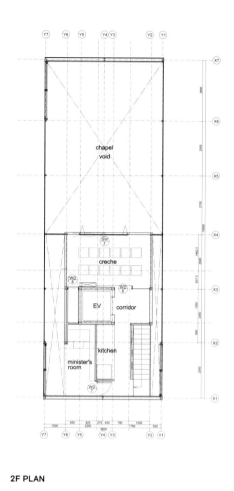

2F PLAN

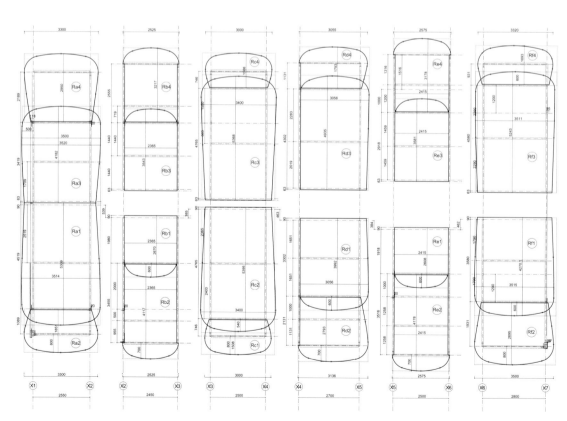

DEVELOPED ROOF PLAN

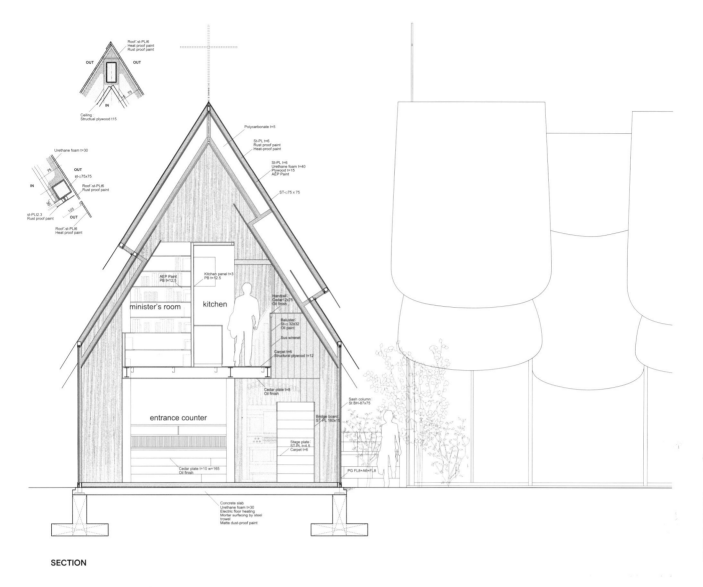

SECTION

This small Protestant church is located in Higashi Totsuka, Kanagawa. For this project, I envisioned a building with the lightness of a cloud that would convey a link to the sky. The cloud-like roof, made by combining 24 plates but leaving gaps between them, has an impressive appearance, causing the building to stand out from its surroundings while also creating a vaguely house-like atmosphere. Under the white roof, there are places with various scales that make the most of the wooden texture. Protected by the roof, the surrounding greenery, and a wall, the building is expansive and open to the town, and functions as a gathering place. Rather than benches, the seating in the chapel is designed to accommodate individual people and can be rearranged according to the occasion. It is an archetypal gathering place with an unprecedented lightness arising from the fact that the church was built in Japan, a country with a lifestyle that is closely connected to gardens and the outdoors. It is my hope that this place will not only be used for religious worship and ceremonies, but a variety of other gatherings involving local residents.

神奈川県東戸塚に建つ小さなプロテスタントの教会である。雲のように軽やかで、空との関係を感じさせる、明るい場所をイメージした。24枚のプレートを、隙間を空けながら組み合わせた雲のような屋根は、周囲から浮き立った印象的な外観をつくると同時に、どことなく家のようでもある。この白い屋根の下に、木の素材感を生かしたさまざまなスケールの場所が展開している。それは屋根と周囲の緑や塀に守られつつも、開放的に街へと開かれた、人びとの集まりのための場所である。礼拝堂の椅子は、ベンチではなく個別のものをデザインし、用途に応じて配置を変えられるようにしている。庭や外部と連続する生活像を育んできた日本に建つ教会だからこそ生まれた、かつてなく軽やかで、原型的な集いの場である。この場所で、礼拝や祝典だけでなく、街の人びとも巻き込んださまざまな集まりが営まれることを願っている。

Higashi-Totsuka Church

Higashi-Totsuka Church

House H

2004-

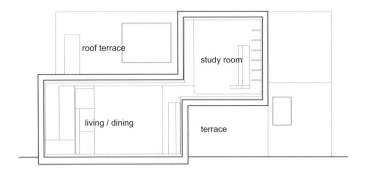
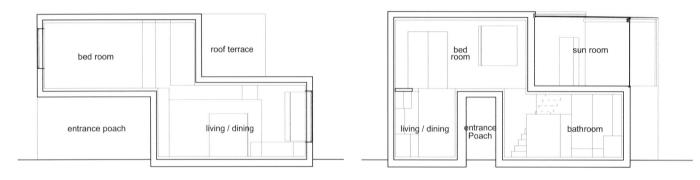
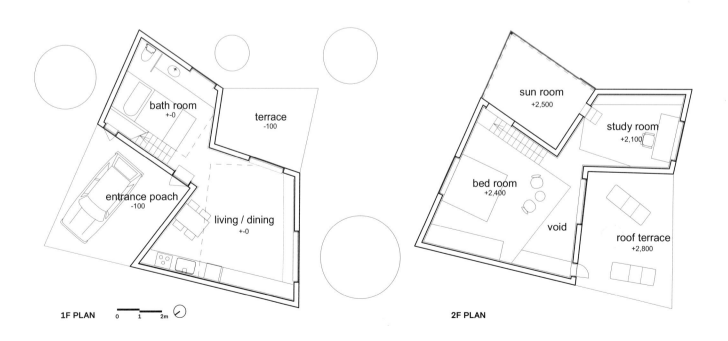

This small house was designed for a married couple. I conceived of a space that was unified in the manner of a single room while maintaining a sense of distance between the residents. It reminded me of a section of cabbage. The gaps between the leaves are connected to form a whole, but each part seems to be independent. If you try to imagine going inside the gaps, you realize that there is no straight sightline that allows you to see into the whole. It is a flexible space in which a differential sightline connects at a slant in each case. While the residents share a single space and sense each other's presence, an appropriate distance is maintained, bringing them in and out of view. Though the space is contiguous and connected, it does allow a sweeping view. This lack of visibility enhances the sense that the residents are simultaneously dwelling in the space. This is a proposal for a residential environment with a new type of comfort that is not exactly one room nor a cluster of rooms.

夫婦ふたりのための小さな住宅である。ワンルーム的な一体空間でありながらも互いに心地良い距離が保てるような場所、それはキャベツの断面のような空間ではないかと考えた。葉と葉に挟まれた間隙は、面的に連続しながらも、それぞれの部分が独立しているように見える。仮にその隙間に入ったことを想像してみるなら、そこには全体を見通すことのできる直線的な視線は存在しないことがわかる。そこは微分的な視線がその都度斜めに連続していくようなたわんだ空間である。住人同士がひとつの空間を共有し、お互いの気配を感じながらも、互いの姿は見え隠れするような適切な距離が担保され、そこには地続きで連続しているが、一望できない空間がある。見えないことによって、住人同士はかえってその空間に同時に存在していることを強く感じるだろう。ワンルームとも、複数の部屋の集合体ともつかない新しい快適さをもった居住環境の提案である。

Masuya
桝屋本店

2005-2006, Niigata, Japan

This is a showroom for small farming equipment, such as Honda's general-purpose machinery, which was built in Niigata. I set out to artificially create a place with a kind of natural environment that people would instinctively be drawn to. The building was made by simply cutting concrete walls with a five-meter grid at the appropriate slant. The slanted opening, inclined at a 45-degree angle, creates a world that is completely different from one based on conventional horizontal and vertical order. If you think of obstruction as the "off" mode and connection as the "on," the slanted line contains an infinite harmony of offs and ons. When you walk inside the building, these elements converge and expand in three dimensions. Because the distant lines move slowly and the close ones quickly, their superposition gives rise to an unexpectedly complex effect. Like a natural environment, the space appeals to our animal instinct. In this work, I attempted to use a distinct method to create a space akin to the human body, equipped with a fluid three-dimensionality unrestricted by a plan, and an integrated space encompassing a complex distance.

新潟に建つホンダ汎用機を中心とした小型農機具のためのショールームである。人が本能的に興味を感じる自然環境のような場所を人工的につくり出すことを考えた。5mグリッドのコンクリート壁を適宜斜めにカットするだけの所作でこの建築はできている。しかし、平面的に45度振れた斜めの開口は従来のような水平・垂直の秩序とはまったく違う世界をつくり出す。遮断されることをOFF、接続していることをONとすればこの斜めのラインはONからOFFへの無限の諧調を含んでいる。内部を歩くと、それらが立体的に輻輳しながら展開することになる。遠くのラインはゆっくり、近くのラインは早く動くから、その重ね合わせは予想もつかない複雑な効果を生む。まさに自然環境のような、人間の動物的な部分に訴えかける空間である。複雑な距離を内包した一体的な空間、プランというツールに縛られない動的な立体性を持った身体に近い空間を、明晰な方法でつくることを意図した。

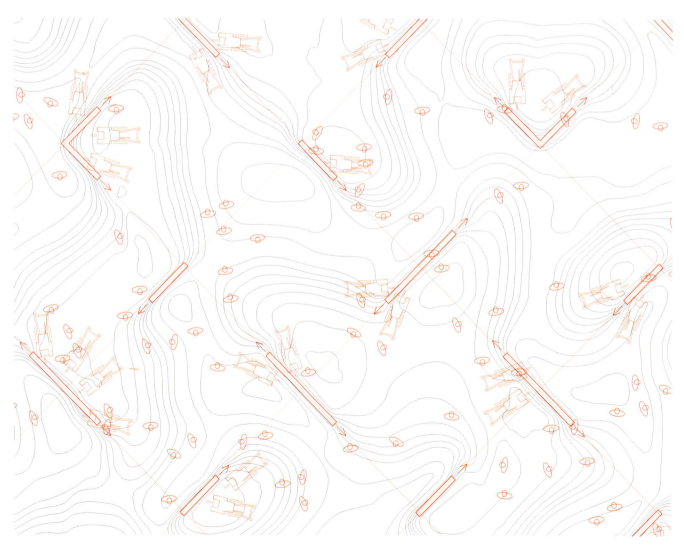

DIAGRAM

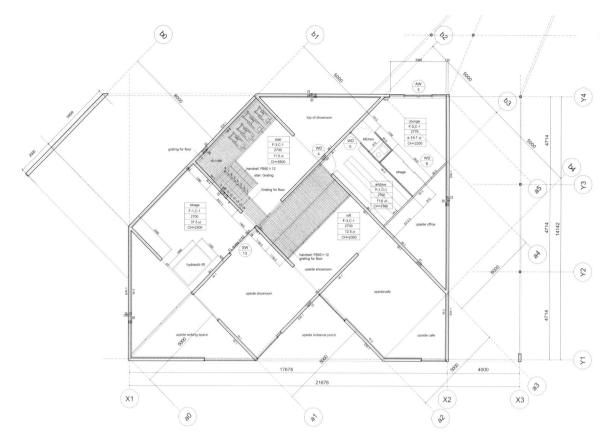

2F PLAN

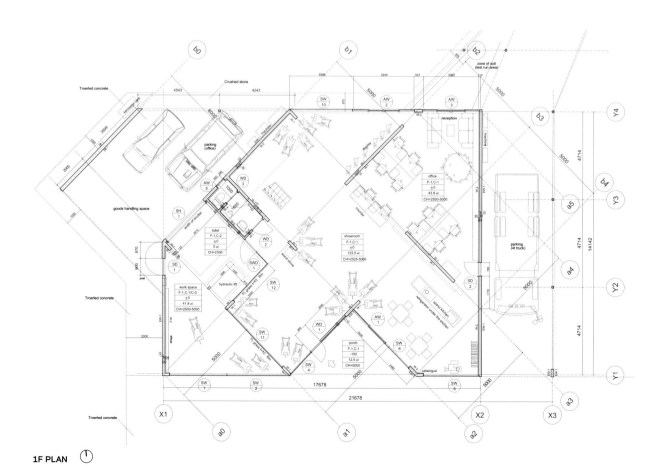

1F PLAN

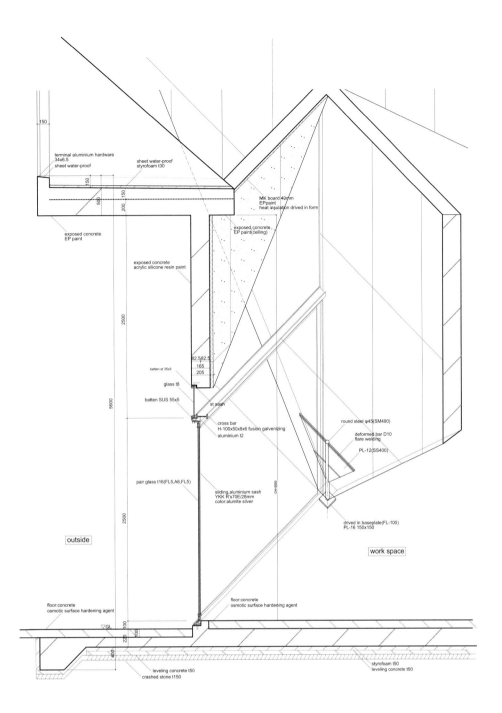

DETAILED SECTION

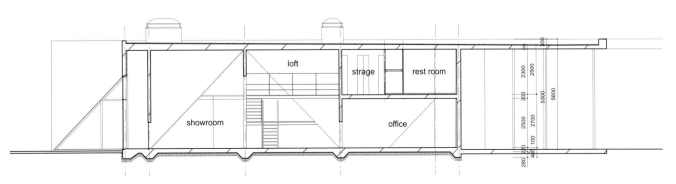

SECTION

Bloomberg Pavilion

2010–2011, Tokyo, Japan

Bloomberg Pavilion

This small pavilion stood for a limited time at the Museum of Contemporary Art Tokyo. I came up with the idea of gradually eliminating the pleats from the building's walls, which rose up straight from the ground, as they extended upward and covering the structure like a tree. Equipped with a kind of leafy shade, the place functioned as a gallery. It had no roof in the conventional sense of the word. While a top light provided shelter from the rain, the pleats, an extension of the walls, had a symbolic appearance akin to a roof. The pleats blocked the sunlight and also functioned as reflectors, inviting soft light into the interior. In other words, the traditional function of the roof was isolated and diffused. Liberated from function, the roof-like element was imbued with an unprecedented degree of freedom from structural restrictions. Making use of a geometrical form known as a "high plane," based on isosceles triangles, the pleats, made of 1.6mm steel plates, swayed gently like a tree in the breeze. How far do the roof and walls extend? How much freedom does architecture have to create a place with a new quality? These are the kind of questions that the pavilion poses.

東京都現代美術館に期間限定で建てられた小さなパビリオンである。地上からまっすぐ建ち上がった壁が、上に行くにつれて次第にひだをなし、建物を覆う樹木のようなものになることを考えた。こうしてできた木陰のような場所が、展示空間になる。ここには従来のような意味での屋根がない。雨をよける機能はトップライトが担っている一方で、壁の延長としてのひだが屋根のようにシンボリックに見える。ひだは日射を遮り、室内にやわらかい光をもたらすリフレクターでもある。これは、従来の屋根の機能が分離し、拡散したともいえる。機能から開放された「屋根のようなもの」は、かつてなく構造的制約から自由だ。ハイプレインと呼ばれる二等辺三角形の幾何学を駆使し、1.6mmの鉄板によってつくられたひだは、風が吹けば樹木のようにやわらかく揺れる。建築物にとってどこまでが屋根であり、壁なのだろうか。新しい質の場所をつくり出すために、建築はどこまで自由になることができるのだろうか。このパビリオンは、そういう問いに開かれている。

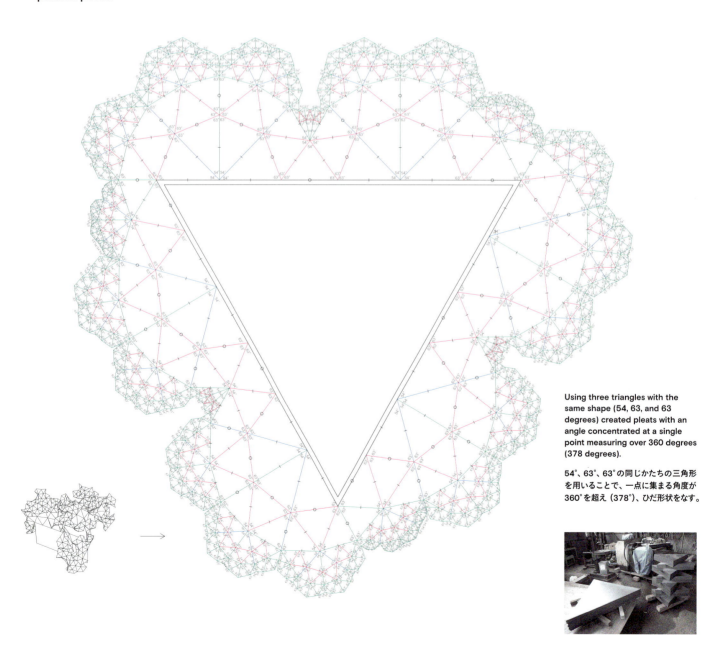

Using three triangles with the same shape (54, 63, and 63 degrees) created pleats with an angle concentrated at a single point measuring over 360 degrees (378 degrees).

54°、63°、63°の同じかたちの三角形を用いることで、一点に集まる角度が360°を超え（378°）、ひだ形状をなす。

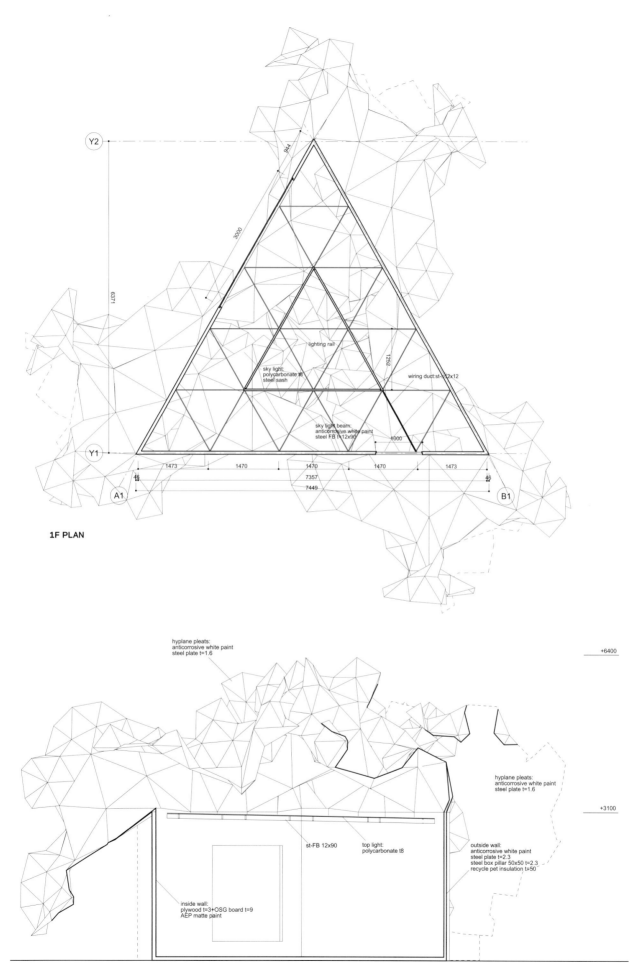

Bloomberg Pavilion

Photosynthesis

2010-2011, Milan, Italy

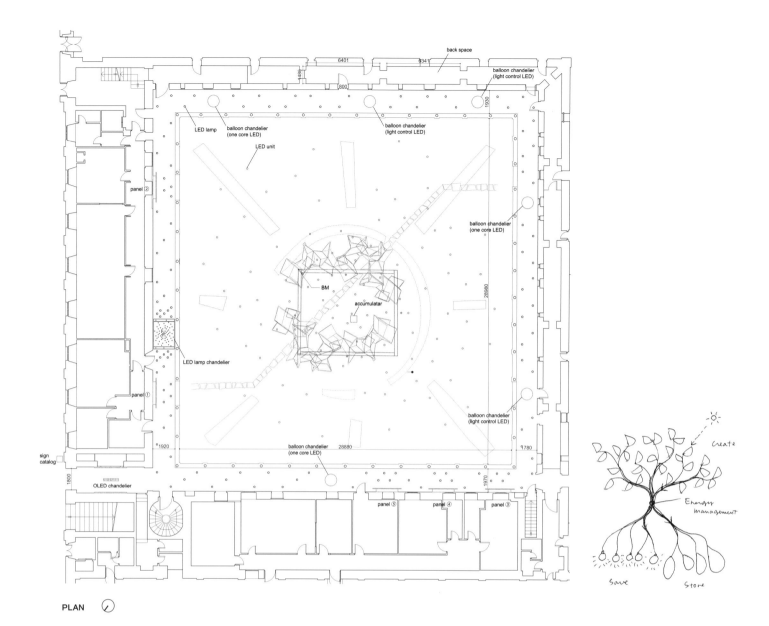

PLAN

This installation was made for the Panasonic display at Salone del Mobile.Milano in 2012. In this design, I attempted to express the process of making, storing, and using energy with an open network based on circulation and interrelation. Using solar panels as "leaves" to generate energy, I created a pavilion that recalled a tree in a courtyard, and imagined that the energy produced there would be sent to the surrounding circuits. Solar panels are normally placed in a flat (two-dimensional) position like turf or moss covering the surface of the ground. In this case, however, I came up with a new arrangement that resembled a tree with an order of three-dimensional "leaves." At first glance, this arrangement might seem irrational, but when you consider the effect of diffused light and the probability of cloudy skies, the panels function almost the same as they would in a flat position. Floating up in the air, the "leaves" were supported by a transparent, polycarbonate structure, and the plants in the courtyard, people, the surrounding facade, and lights were randomly reflected on the shiny resin surface. In this historical setting, I attempted to create a new landscape by reinterpreting nature.

2012年のミラノサローネにおいてパナソニックのために考えたインスタレーションである。エネルギーをつくり、蓄え、使う、という流れで循環し、互いに関係し合う開かれたネットワークを表現することを試みた。エネルギーをつくり出す「葉」としての太陽光パネルを用いて、中庭に樹木のようなパビリオンをつくり、ここで生み出されたエネルギーが、周囲の回廊に送り出されることをイメージした。太陽光パネルは通常平面的（二次元的）に敷き詰められ、植物でいえば地面を覆う芝やコケのような使われ方をするが、ここでは三次元的な「葉」の秩序をもった樹木のような新しいパネルの配置を考えた。立体的な配置は一見不合理に見えるが、拡散光の効果や曇天の確率などを考慮することで、平面配置とほぼ同等の働きが可能となる。空中に浮遊する「葉」は透明なポリカーボネート構造によって支えられ、きらきらとした樹脂の表面には中庭の植物や人びと、周囲のファサードや照明などがランダムに映り込む。歴史的な佇まいの中に、自然を再解釈した新しい風景がつくり出された。

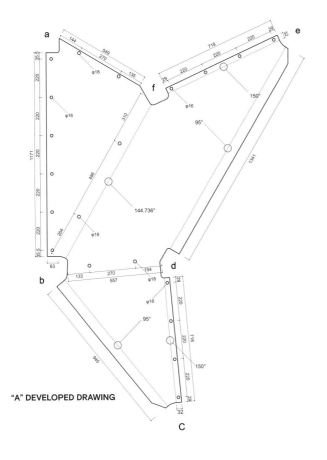

"A" DEVELOPED DRAWING

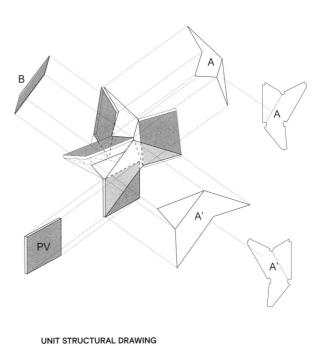

UNIT STRUCTURAL DRAWING

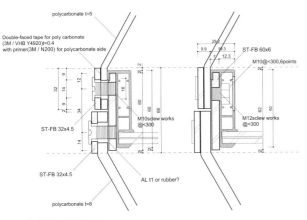

DETAILED SECTION

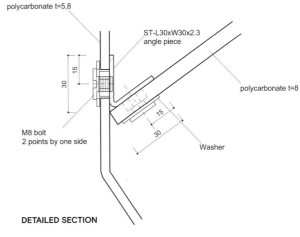

DETAILED SECTION

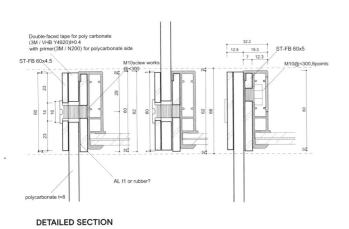

DETAILED SECTION

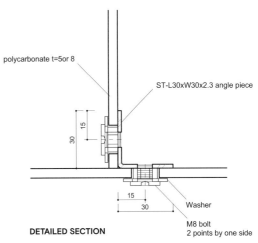

DETAILED SECTION

Photosynthesis

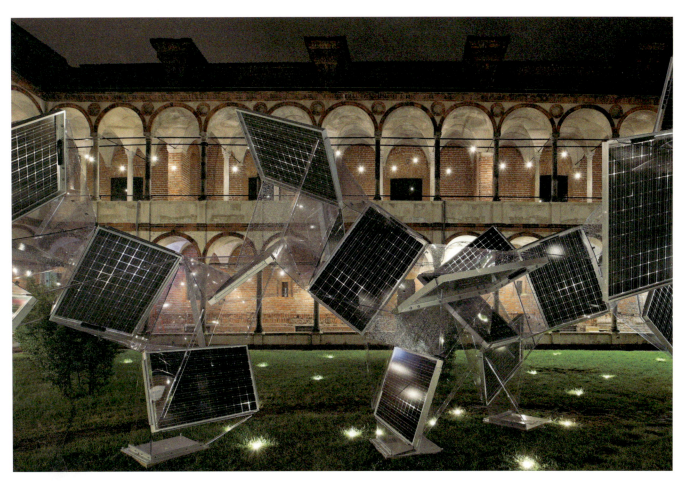

Photosynthesis

173

Long House

2011-

SITE PLAN 0 2 5 10m

SECTION

This vacation home stands along Chile's Pacific Coast. For this project, I conceived of architecture as something that would connect various territories, scattered across the entire site in this uncommon location, like smoke, a stretch of road, or a plant attached to the terrain. It is an organic building that grew out of shapeless elements such as the various desires that emerged from the dialogue and relationship between the site and the surrounding environment. I repeatedly adjusted things as I considered a variety of factors that were entangled there. These included the general arrangement of the places, a necessity in a residential area, the three-dimensional placement of the road connecting them, the omission or obstruction of sight lines, the creation of places that would be protected from sea breezes, and the relationship between the adjacent properties and the estimated volume. While remaining distinctly aware of the fact that even a slight change in position or form would create a completely different relationship, I arrived at the final shape after conducting wind simulations and other tests. This work is a statement that expresses the value of new architecture, and at the same time, a comfortable house that frees the spirit.

チリの太平洋に面した海岸に建つセカンドハウスである。類まれな場所を前にして、敷地全体に散らばるさまざまなテリトリーを結びつける、煙のような、引き伸ばされた道のような、地形にへばりついた植物のような存在が、ここでの建築だと考えた。敷地や周辺環境との対話から生まれたさまざまな欲望やそれらの関係性といった、かたちのないものからはじまる有機的な建築。住宅の中で必要とされる場所の大まかな配置からはじめて、それらを結びつける立体的な道の配置、視線の抜けや遮断、強い海風から守られた場所をつくること、隣地に想定されているボリュームとの関係など、お互いにからまり合うさまざまなファクターを同時に考えながら調整を繰り返す。ほんのわずかな配置や形状の違いが、まったく違った関係性をつくり出すことを明晰に意識しながら、風のシミュレーションなども合わせて、最終形状を浮かび上がらせている。これは新しい建築の価値観を示すステートメントであり、同時に精神を開放する快適な住宅である。

Long House

PLAN

SECTION

Long House
181

9hours Project

2016–2018, Japan

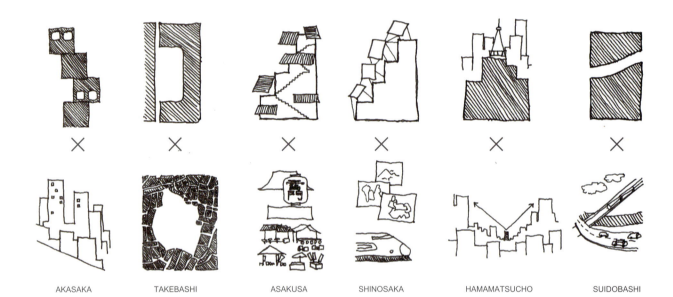

| AKASAKA | TAKEBASHI | ASAKUSA | SHINOSAKA | HAMAMATSUCHO | SUIDOBASHI |

This was a project for a new type of capsule-hotel chain that is spreading throughout central Tokyo. These are not the kind of capsules that are part of a self-sufficient system akin to the proposals that emerged during the Metabolist architecture era. Instead, by connecting with a variety of external elements that are directly exposed to the city, the capsules are adapted in parallel to individual entities in the contemporary sense of the word. The capsules have a micro-scale, equal to half a floor height, and they can be adjusted to fit into any kind of gap in the city, thriving freely like a slime mold. The characteristics of the surrounding urban area crossbreed with this aggregation of capsules to produce places unlike any other. The capsules, which become entangled with the city on two levels, have been unleashed in the Akasaka, Takebashi, Asakusa neighborhoods of Tokyo as well as in Shin-Osaka and Nagoya, functioning like a reverberating sound source that renews the image of urban living.

東京を中心に幅広く展開する新感覚のカプセルホテルチェーンのプロジェクトである。ここでカプセルはメタボリズム建築の時代に発案されたような自己完結したシステムの一部では、もはやない。それは都市に直接さらされ、さまざまな外的要素とつながっていくものとして、言い換えるなら今日的な意味合いでの個の存在とパラレルなものとして、換骨奪胎されている。カプセルはまた、階高の半分のマイクロスケールをもち、都市のどんな隙間にでも自在なかたちで入り込み、はびこる、いわば「粘菌」のような自由な存在である。そうして生まれたカプセルの集合体に、周辺の都市の特徴が掛け合わされ、それぞれ、他のどこにもない場所となる。この、二重の意味で都市とからみ合うカプセルたちは、東京の赤坂、竹橋、浅草、さらには新大阪、名古屋などへと解き放たれ、都市生活のイメージを更新する響きの音源となるだろう。

9hours Takebashi
9hours 竹橋

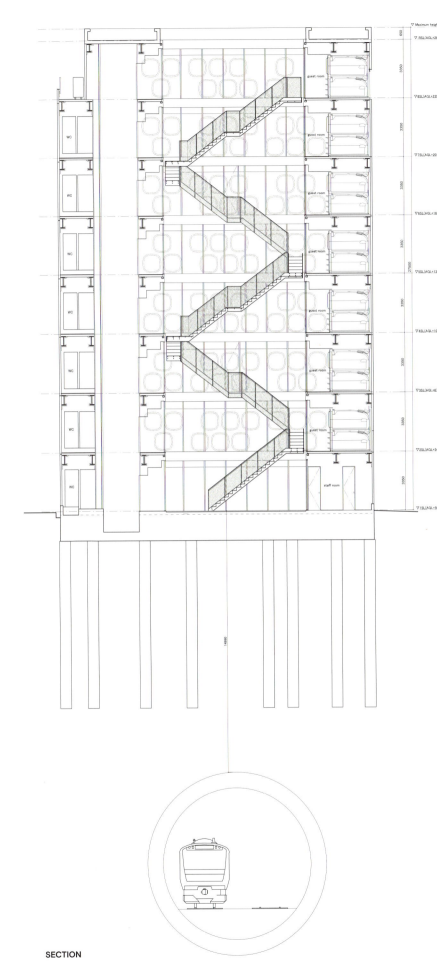

SECTION

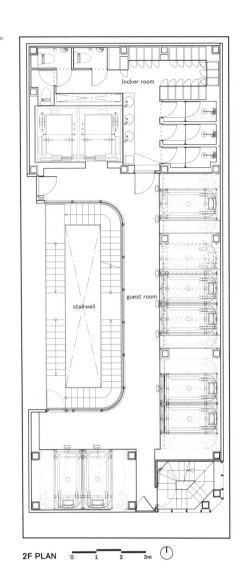

2F PLAN

9hours Project

9hours Akasaka
9hours 赤坂

2F PLAN

1F PLAN

B1F PLAN

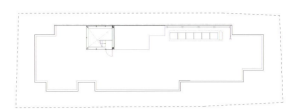
RF PLAN

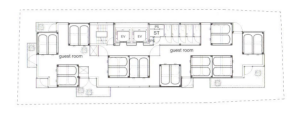
4F PLAN

3F PLAN

9hours Asakusa
9hours 浅草

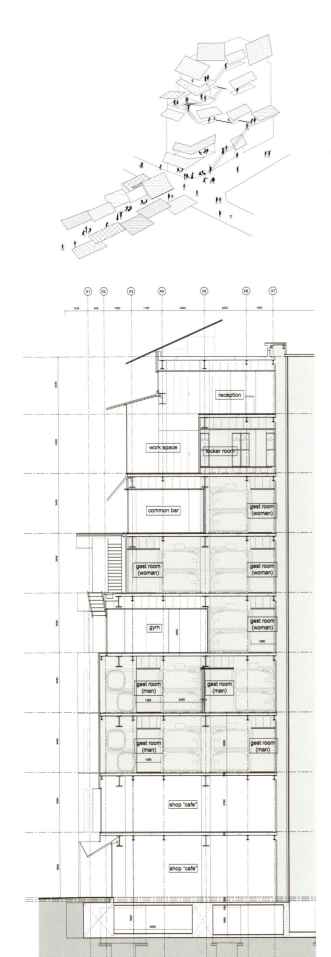

SECTION

9F PLAN

7F PLAN

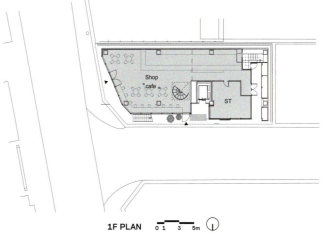

1F PLAN

9hours Project

9hours Shin-Osaka
9hours 新大阪

9hours Hamamatsucho
9hours 浜松町

Discovering New Commitment

Pan Locality

Imagining life without tomatoes[1] is difficult for Japanese people, as it is for people worldwide. But it has been only 500 years since this plant originated in the Andes and was brought to Europe. Its hardiness and its compatibility with various recipes have given it worldwide appeal over a very short period of time.

there are species that have spread all over the world even without the human intervention that the tomato has enjoyed. But perhaps, or almost certainly, these species have evolved in some special circumstances, that is to say they have evolved in a local relationship and should have come into existence. Things arising locally are spreading globally, or they are growing into the basis for something universal.

But this is not limited to species: the same may be true of food, clothing, ideas, and architecture.

The Locality of *Tangle tab*

Among the spatial characteristics of traditional Japanese architecture is division of spaces without clear definition of boundaries. Without clear enclosures as in Western architecture, there are layers of ambiguous boundaries that can be activated or deactivated with architectural elements. At the boundary between exterior and interior there is something like an edge zone, where inside and outside are defined by fences, eaves and so forth. Upholding this architectural style is a wooden framework employing only a minimum of walls, creating spaces that enable air to flow through, suiting the country's warm and humid climate. These aspects of Japanese architecture have often been pointed out, but it seems this outlook can be expanded to encompass the entirety of East Asia and extend to contemporary as well as traditional architecture. First of all, the spatial characteristic of ambiguous boundaries applies to many countries along the Pacific Rim in East Asia. Although this region extends across a wide climatic zone, from just south of the equator to latitude 40°N, it is all a temperate zone with heavy rainfall, belonging to the so-called "Asian monsoon region."

It is also home to a variant of regionally cultivated architecture of *tangle tab* that lacks clear enclosures. If 20th-century modern architecture addressed the concept of clearly enclosed "spaces," *tangle tab* is a new concept for defining "places" without clear enclosures. However, it is also an architectural variant with the same roots as the spaces nurtured in the East Asian climate, and it is related to the universalization of the local.

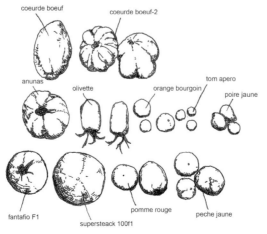

[1] tomatoes

汎ローカリティー

トマト[1]のない生活を想像することは、日本人にとってすら難しい。しかしアンデス原産のこの植物が、ヨーロッパに持ち込まれてからまだ500年ほどしかたっていないのだ。トマトのもつ種としてのたくましさと、さまざまな調理法を可能にするキャパシティーのようなものが、ごく短い期間に世界的な広がりを獲得したのだ。

トマトのように人が介在していなくても、世界中にその分布を広げている生物種がある。しかし、多分というかほぼ確実に、その生物種は何らかの特殊条件のなかで、つまりはあるローカルな関係性のなかで進化を遂げ、今日の姿になったはずである。そしてローカルから生まれ出たものが、グローバルに広がっていく。あるいは何らかの普遍性をもった、ベースとなる存在になる。

しかしこれは、生物種に限った話ではない。恐らくは料理も、衣服も、思想も、そして建築もまた、そのようなものなのである。

からまりしろのローカリティー

日本建築の空間特性として、境界がはっきり定まらないような空間の区切り方がある。西洋建築のようにはっきりとしたエンクロージャーをもたないで、建具によって接続も切断も可能な曖昧な境界が重層している。外部と内部の境界には縁のような場所があり、また庇や軒によって規定される中間的な領域が内外をつないでいる。こうした建築様式を支えているのは最小限の壁だけで成立する木造の架構であり、境界をまたいで空気が流れていく空間は、温暖で多湿な気候風土によく適合している。こうしたことは日本建築に対してしばしば指摘されてきたが、東アジア全体まで視野を広げて、現代建築をめぐる問題意識を拡張することは可能ではないか。そもそも、境界が曖昧な空間特性は、東アジアの太平洋の縁に沿って展開しているさまざまな国々で見られる特性である。赤道直下から北緯40度に至るまでかなり広範な気候帯に分布しているとはいえ、いわゆる「アジアモンスーン地域」に属した、雨が多く温暖な場所であることは共通している。

このような地域で育まれてきた、明確なエンクロージャーをもたない建築の変種が、〈からまりしろ〉の建築だともいえる。20世紀の近代建築が掲げた概念が、明確なエンクロージャーをもった「空間」だったとするなら、〈からまりしろ〉とは明確なエンクロージャーではない仕方で場所を定義する新しい概念である。しかし、それは同時に東アジアの気候風土に育まれた建築空間と同じルーツをもつ変種であって、ローカルなものの普遍化と関係している。

[2] Taipei Roofs (2013-18)

Increasing Density in East Asia

Taipei Roofs[2] (2013-18, p. 212) is a 12-story apartment building built on a site near a shopping area in Taipei, Taiwan. As a project, it could have been what we call a "tower mansion" in Japan. These high-rise apartment buildings are typical 20th-century structures and their lineage is unrelated to the East Asian tradition. Meanwhile, throughout Taiwan you can see people enjoying meals and conversation in simple places that are extensions of the street. We sought to design a 21st-century high-rise apartment building suited to the East Asian lifestyle. It has a set-back volume with large terraces on each floor, their roofs covered with trees. The roofs create a comfortable space protected from strong sunlight and rain, and their eaves connect to create a three-dimensional intermediate area. It is a *tangle tab* of water and wind where rainwater is effectively diverted and wind from above is divided into separate air flows for comfort.

Archipelagoes

As you can see on a map, East Asia is an interface with the Pacific Ocean on the edge of the Eurasian continent and forms an archipelago[3] with a large number of peninsulas and island chains. It is a region rich in marine areas that serve as transit zones or intermediate zones. We can say that the tradition of thin-enclosure architecture arose in this region, and the same can be said of the *tangle tab* concept. This is the nature of human thought, or of architecture, which is forced to take place within a certain locality.
However, because they evolve out of local relationships that spread among all species throughout the earth, even ideas nurtured by specific regional conditions have a kind of universality and can evolve into something powerful and applicable in other regions. While there may be continentally universal ideas, on the other hand, archipelagic ideas also have some universality.

[3] archipelagoes

東アジア的高密度化

　富富話合[2]（2013-18, p.212）は台湾台北市のショッピングエリアに近い敷地に建つ地上12階建ての集合住宅である。与件としてはいわゆるタワーマンションのひとつになることが想像できた。周知のようにこうしたタワーマンションは典型的な20世紀型の建築であって、東アジア的伝統とは異なる系列の空間であるといってよい。一方、台湾の街の至る所で、道の延長上にある簡素な場所で、食事や会話を楽しむ人びとの姿を見ることができる。こうした東アジア的生活像にふさわしい21世紀の高層集合住宅を考えようと、私たちは試みた。セットバックするボリューム形状によって、各階に大きなテラスをつくり、それらが屋根か樹木によって覆われている。屋根は、強い日差しや強い雨から守られた快適な場所をつくり出すとともに、全体としてそれぞれの屋根の下がつながった、立体的な中間領域が生まれる。それは雨水を首尾よく流し、上空の風を快適に分岐させる、水や風の〈からまりしろ〉なのである。

アーキペラゴ

　地図上の東アジアを見るとわかるように、それはユーラシア大陸の縁に展開する太平洋とのインターフェースであって、おびただしい半島と島々によるアーキペラゴ（群島）[3] をなす。海という交通空間、あるいは中間領域だらけの地域なのである。エンクロージャーが希薄な建築の伝統は、このようなローカリティーから生まれたといってよい。そしてまた、〈からまりしろ〉という考え方も同様である。それは、何らかのローカリティーのもとに思考することを余儀なくされている、人間の思考あるいは建築というものの性なのではないだろうか。

　しかし、地球全体に広がった生命種がもとはあるローカルな関係性から進化したように、ある地域条件によって育まれた考え方が、ある種の普遍性をもち、他の地域でも通用するような野太いものに鍛え上げられることはあり得る。大陸的な普遍性の思考があったとすれば、他方でアーキペラゴ的な思考もある普遍性をもつ。

Earth

In any art, regardless of country, there may be a fermentation process that transforms the elements (earth, minerals, plants, and so on) making up the surface of the earth. In particular, this is true for art that reflects the characteristics of the local soil. For example, I wonder if the reason the folding screen *Kakitsubata-zu*[4] (Irises) conveys a distinctively Japanese atmosphere and feeling, despite the universality of its dry and graphic methodology, is closely related to something emanated by the minerals used[5].

Katsuei Misawa, a geographer who lived around a century ago, said that the climate is where the surface of the earth and the bottom of the atmosphere come in contact. From this radical standpoint, the "surface phenomena" caused by contact between earth and atmosphere, including human activities, are all part of the geography field. Not only the roofs of private houses but even that of the stationery shop by the local elementary school are "surface phenomena."

However, Misawa says that architecture is a purely cultural phenomenon unrelated to climate, and is not a surface phenomenon. This definition is clearly understandable with regard to specific, typical cases. However, the boundaries and critical points separating the two are ambiguous, almost indistinguishable. And new architecture is always headed toward a critical point between natural / artificial and unconscious / conscious.

Transformation of Soil

Architecture like that of the Yaodong[6] clay plateau in China could be regarded as transfiguration of soil, like the earth's elements solidified. This could be called a classic surface phenomenon.

What of the Roman concrete used to build Rome? Structures made from pozzolanic (volcanic) ash mined from beneath Rome were constructed using certain chemical reactions on the earth's surface. And the concrete used to construct modern cities? Concrete, made by solidifying sand, cement and aggregates obtainable in each region is a standardized material, but it is also earth in altered form. Now, we may be entering territory that no longer relates to surface phenomena. However, whether it is a surface phenomenon or not, it is certainly a transfiguration of earth.

What of trees? We can say that the terrain shaped by the flow of water (= earth) and the shapes of trees releasing moisture into the air are the same. So, what should we think of architecture that proclaims itself similar to a tree? Can we call it, too, a transfiguration of earth? If so, is it among the surface phenomena? Does that mean it is already outside the realm of architecture?

Architecture & Fungi

Shinohara Kazuo said that a private house is like a mushroom. This is almost synonymous with saying that a private house is a "surface phenomenon." And for Shinohara mushrooms, or surface phenomena, were distinct from "architecture" as a conscious or cultural human activity. Shinohara says that while human activities may unconsciously play a part in surface phenomena, this is not synonymous with architecture.

[4] Kakitsubata-zu

[5] marachite

土

どの国のどんなアートであろうと、極言すれば、地表面を構成する要素（土、鉱物、植物など）を変容させた〈発酵〉ものなのだといえなくもない。とりわけ、あるローカルな地表面の特性が色濃く反映されたものについてはそうである。たとえば、「燕子花図屏風」[4] が、ドライでグラフィカルな方法論のもつ普遍性とは別に、そこはかとなく日本的な空気感をまとうのは、そのマチエールをなす鉱物[5] が放つものと色濃く関係しているのではないだろうか。

風土とは大地の表面と大気の底面との触れ合う接触面のことだ、と述べたのは、今からおよそ100年前を生きた地理学者、三沢勝栄である。このようなラディカルな観点のもとでは、大地と大気の接触によって起こる「地表現象」は、人間の活動も含めて、すべて地理学の対象になる。民家の屋根はもちろん、小学校脇の文房具屋でさえ、地表現象なのである。

しかし風土と無関係な、純粋に文化的な現象としての建築は、地表現象ではない、と三沢は述べる。このような定義は、それぞれのティピカルなケースにおいてはわかりやすい。しかし、両者の境目、臨界点はほとんど見分けがつかない曖昧なものになるだろう。そして新しい建築の方向性は、常にこの自然／人工あるいは無意識／意識のクリティカルポイントに向かっているわけである。

土の変容体

たとえば中国、黄土高原のヤオトン[6] のような建築は、大地の成分がそのまま固まったような〈土〉の変容体であって、典型的な地表現象だといえるだろう。

ローマの街をつくっているローマン・コンクリートはどうだろうか。ローマの地下から採掘された火山灰、ポッツォラーナを原料としてできた建造物は、地表面のある種の化学反応によってできたものではないだろうか。現代都市をつくっているコンクリートはどうか。地域ごとに手に入る砂やセメント、骨材を固めてつくったコンクリートは、標準化されているとはいえ、やはり〈土〉の変容体といってもいいものではないだろうか。いや、もはやここまでくれば、地表現象とはいえないものの領域に足を踏み入れているのだろうか。しかし、地表現象なのかどうかはともかくも、少なくともそれは〈土〉の変容体には違いない。

樹木はどうだろうか。水の流れによってフラクタルな樹形をなす地形＝〈土〉と、空中に水分を解き放つ樹形は、同じものだとはいえないだろうか。では、樹のような存在であることを標榜する建築はどうだろうか。それは〈土〉の変容体だといえるだろうか。だとすればそれは、地表現象の一部なのだろうか。とはいえそれはすでに、建築と呼べるものではなくなっているのだろうか。

建築／きのこ

篠原一男は、民家はきのこである、と言った。これは、民家は地表現象である、と言うのとほぼ同義である。そして、篠原にとって、きのこ、あるいは地表現象は人間の意識的、文化的営為としての「建築」とは異なるものだったのである。地表現象の一部を人間の営みが無意識的に担うとしても、それは建築ではない、と篠原は言う。

しかし21世紀に新しく発見されるべき建築のありようは、自然と人工、あるいは意識的なものと無意識的なも

However, the new architecture to be discovered in the 21st century will surely incorporate nature and artifice, conscious and unconscious, and the criticality of the human-animal boundary. For example, it will inquire into the nature of architecture as a surface phenomenon.

The Intertexture of earth

However, it seems that climate and surface phenomena and intentional human activities (especially cultural ones) are not irrelevant to begin with, but have been entangled in complex ways––as in the *Kakitsubata-zu* (Irises) folding screen.
Museum Forest of *"Hill Valley"* (2014-, p. 220) was a catalyst for thought about such things. Among Taiwan's relatively new cities, Tainan is recognized as the oldest. Taiwan's first massive, largely brick castle was built there in 1624 by the Dutch as an office for the Governor General. Today it is partially eroded partly by plants and has the air of a ruin. In Tainan there are many other historic brick buildings, and the texture of red brick is fundamental to the city's atmosphere. Red plaster walls, such as those of Confucian temples[7], are also a common sight and characterize the texture of Tainan. In other words, the red clay used to make bricks is responsible for both the exotic and the indigenous aspects of the city. And entangled in the half-crumbled brick walls of Tainan's ruins are plants such as banyan. The image of brick structures returning to nature is associated with that of subtropical vegetation. Brick evokes intertwined visions of conflict between the natural and the artificial, robust vegetation, and the fertile soil and rain that are its prerequisites.
The brick-based texture of earth evokes various contexts and historical implications unique to Tainan. In the *Hill Valley* proposal, we proposed "hills" and "valleys" raised from the earth's surface in Tainan, in other words an altered form of soil combining building and earth's surface, for the art museum. In creating contemporary architecture that is a surface phenomenon and has contact with Tainan culture, earth is a kind of hinge that interlaces the unconscious world and conscious worlds.
If the architecture I create is somehow a transformed form of earth, then it may serve as a hinge that connects architecture, which has approached the human from an inhuman angle, to the human once again.

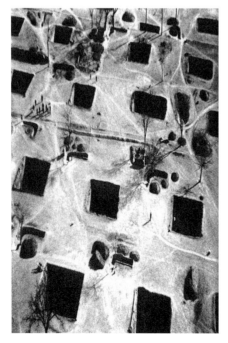

[6] Yaodong

の、人間と動物の境界のクリティカリティーに触れるだろう。たとえば、地表現象としての建築はどのようなものなのかを問うこと。

〈土〉のインターテクスチャリティー

しかしそもそも、風土とか地表現象と、人間の意識的な活動（とりわけ文化的なもの）とは、無関係なものではなく、複雑にからみ合い続けてきたのではないだろうか。「燕子花図屏風」がそうであったように。

台南市美術館"丘谷之森"（2014-, p. 220）は、そのようなことを考えるきっかけになった。台南は、比較的歴史の浅い台湾の都市の中で、もっとも歴史をもつ古都として認識されている。1624年、最初に総督府が置かれた台南に、オランダによって築かれた最初の城は、レンガを多用したマッシブな建造物であった。現在は植物によって一部浸食されていて、廃墟としての存在感を放っている。台南にはこのほかにもレンガを用いた歴史的建造物が多く、赤レンガの質感が、街の印象と結び付いている。また、孔子廟[7]に見られるような赤い漆喰の壁もしばしば見られ、台南の街のテクスチュアを特徴付けている。つまり、外来性と土着性の両面性を、レンガの赤い土が担っている。加えて、台南の廃墟では、ガジュマルのような樹木が、半ば崩れ落ちたレンガの壁面にからまっている。レンガの組石が自然に還る過程のイメージが、亜熱帯の植生と結びついている。つまりレンガという素材を通して自然と人工の拮抗やたくましい植生、あるいはその前提となる肥沃な土や雨といったものが、ないまぜに想起されるわけである。

レンガによる〈土〉のテクスチャリティーが、台南特有のさまざまな文脈や歴史的含意を呼び寄せている。台南市美術館では、そのような文脈のなかに、台南の地表面から隆起したような「丘」と「谷」、つまり建物と地面が混在する〈土〉の変容体を美術館として提案した。地表現象であるとともに、台南の文化と接点をもつ現代的な建築をつくること。〈土〉というものが、ある種の蝶番となって、無意識の世界と意識の世界を交錯させる。

もし、僕のつくろうとしている建築が、何らかのかたちで〈土〉の変容体であるのなら、「人間」を人間でないものの側からアプローチしてきた建築は、〈土〉のインターテクスチャリティーのようなものを蝶番にして、再び「人間」と出合うことができるのかもしれない。

[7] Confucian temple

Others

Tombs

In the city where I grew up, there were a large number of tombs called the Mozu Burial Mounds. The largest is the Emperor Nintoku Mausoleum[8], on a scale rivaling that of the pyramids and the tombs of the Qin Emperor. However, at eye level there is nothing to distinguish it from other old tumuli (burial mounds): it is an ancient tomb covered in trees, appearing as a low hill, its mysterious shape only visible when seen from above. It is a highly geometric and beautiful archaeological site, which was once covered with shining stones and decorated with regularly arranged clay rings.

When I was a child, there was certainly no mistaking its greatness. At first sight it was somber, and barely revealed its presence except when a marathon was being run around it. But later, its humble appearance obviously differed from nature when examined closely, and despite being covered in trees, it was clearly built on a distinct principle. Perhaps because I knew how it had once looked, I was quietly moved by how its original spirit lingered, even though it was completely covered in greenery. As an architect, I even wanted to design buildings similar to tumuli. That does not mean buildings covered with vegetation. It means architecture that even when exposed to the vagaries of time and the necessities of life so that its original form could hardly be seen, still faintly emanates the spirit in which it was originally constructed.

Rather than having my own lofty, isolated aesthetic, I seek to create structures that will be called beautiful even when, or because, they are filled with various people and things. *Sarugaku* (2006-08, p. 240) is a commercial complex that got me thinking about these things. I imagined people and various things like secretions emerging from each business clinging to the structure.

Origins of the Ego

Sociologist Maki Yusuke refers to various biological findings, and asserts that the process by which the self was acquired in the process of biological evolution included the incorporation

[8] Emperor Nintoku Mausoleum

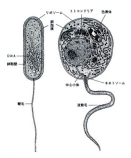

[9] prokaryote / eukaryote

他者

古墳

僕の育った街には、百舌鳥古墳群[8]と呼ばれる古墳が沢山あった。そのなかでも最大の仁徳天皇陵は、規模的にはピラミッドや秦の始皇帝の墓と同規模の巨大なものである。しかし、アイレベルで通り過ぎると、それが古墳であるのかすら、気付かないくらいつつましい。森に覆われ、小高い丘か小さな山のように見える古墳は、上空から見ると初めてその異様な存在感を開示する。それは高度に幾何学的な人工物であり、築造当初は輝く葺石で覆われ、規則正しく並んだ埴輪で飾られた、華やかな存在だった。

しかし子どものころは、それは確かに偉大なものには違いないが、一見すると地味で、たまにマラソンでその周りを一周するくらいの存在にしか見えなかった。しかし後になって、このつつましい外観も、よく見ると明らかに自然物とは異なっており、森に覆われていようとも、そこはかとない原理性を放っていることがわかるようになった。原初の姿を知っているからかもしれないが、完全に苔むしてまでもなお、建造された時の精神が、かすかに、しかしそれゆえに強く漂っていることに静かな感動を覚えた。建築家として、古墳のような建築をつくりたいと思うようにすらなった。緑に覆われた建築という意味ではない。さまざまな時間の経過や生活上の必要にさらされ、元の姿がほとんど見えなくなってしまったとしても、その建築をつくった精神が、かすかに、強く漂うような建築をつくりたいのである。

それは、言い換えるなら、建築がどれだけ多くの〈他者〉を受け入れられるか、という問いとほぼ同値である。自分だけで完結した美学をもつというよりは、そこにやってくるさまざまな事物にほとんど埋め尽くされたとしても、逆にそのことが美しいといえるような建築。

Sarugaku（2006-08, p. 240）はそんなことを考えはじめるきっかけになった商業ビルの複合体である。この建物の表面に、それぞれの店舗からの分泌物のようなさまざまなものや人びとがからまることを想像した。建築物が単独で美しくつくられることの美学ではなく、生物多様性をもった自然の谷のような、生き生きとした〈他者〉たちに覆われた光景を美しい、といえるような価値観を提示したかったのである。

自我の起源

社会学者の真木悠介はさまざまな生物学的な知見を参照しながら、自我というものが生物進化のなかでより高度に獲得されていった過程は、個的なもののなかにより高度に〈他者〉を含み込む過程であったと述べる。たとえば原核生物から真核生物[9]への進化は、ミトコンドリアや葉緑体といった別の生命体を、細胞内に取り入れることによって起こった。リン・マーギュリスが言うように、真核細胞そのものがひとつの共生体なのである。有性生殖による他者性の取り入れや、多細胞生物の体内が微生物の生態系になっていること、進化の過程におけるウイルスの意外に大きな役割など、生物の世界の成り立ちは、他者性の介在なしには説明できないからまり合いに満ちている。

建築というものも、生命の営みとつながるものである以上、同様のことがいえるのではないだろうか。建築の個性のありよう、あるいは建築を設計する思考のありようは、より高度に他者性を含み込んだものになってゆくのではないだろうか。

あらかじめ現実を適切にモデル化する理論を構築し、そのモデルによって新たな現実を適切に制御しようとする思考。それはまさに建築がずっと行ってきたことである。しかし、そのような考え方にとって他者的にはたらく、非理論的なものが、コンピューターの計算処理能力が介在することによって多様に台頭している。

他者的思考

たとえば、〈発酵・浸食〉（p. 109）の項で論じたシミュレーションと最適化を用いた設計手法は、今やほとんどの建築家にとってなじみのあるものとなった。しかしそれが、建築を設計する知的営為の根本の部分を変える潜在力をもつものであることに、もっと多くの注意が払われてよいと思う。なぜならそれは、理論的であること、言い換えるなら、モデル的思考で世界を単純化して読み解こうとする思考形態とまったく異なる、他者性を内包した思考形態を要求するものだからである。

建築構造設計の例を考えてみよう。FEM解析による力の流れや変形のシミュレーションによって、人間の思考に落とし込むためのモデル化、単純化を図らなくても、コンピューターがありのままを計算できてしまうようにな

of others, at a highly sophisticated level, into the individual. For example, the evolution from prokaryotes to eukaryotes[9] occurred through incorporation of other life forms such as mitochondria and chloroplasts into cells. As Margulis says, eukaryotic cells themselves are one symbiotic unit. The incorporation of the other through sexual reproduction, the fact that the interiors of multicellular organisms are microbial ecosystems, the surprisingly significant role of the virus in the process of evolution, the formation of the world of living organisms, cannot be explained without the intervention of otherness.

The same can be said of architecture, as it connects to the activities of life. Architecture's individual character, or the ideas behind architectural design, comes to incorporate otherness in a more sophisticated manner.

The idea is to construct theories that model reality effectively in advance, and use those models to govern new realities effectively. That is exactly what architecture has done throughout history. However, we are seeing the emergence of diverse non-theoretical systems that work in ways alien to this approach through the advance of computers' computational processing capacity.

Alien Thinking

For example, the design methodology employing simulation and optimization, discussed in the section on fermentation & erosion (p. 108), is now familiar to most architects. However, I think much more attention should be paid to its potential to change fundamental aspects of the intellectual activity of architectural design. This is because it is theoretical, in other words, it requires modes of thinking encompassing otherness, which differ completely from modes of thinking that attempt to grasp the world by simplifying it through modeling.

Let us examine an example of architectural structure design. By simulating force flow and deformation through FEM analysis, computers can calculate on their own terms, without modeling and simplifying so as to fit human thought patterns. However, humans cannot trace whether these outcomes are correct or not. Therefore, structure designers compare the results of FEM analysis with results verified using a simpler model that humans can understand. This can be called the most fundamental example of thought that circulates back and forth between hypothesis and external thinking.

In the era of big data and AI, more advanced modes of thought will develop along these lines. This suggests the possibility of new ways of thinking premised on a blend of simple, easily understandable thought and other forms of thought that could be called non-theoretical calculation processes. These non-theoretical calculation processes may also include real, natural phenomena, including the reactions of large numbers of people to specific spatial characteristics and the diverse behaviors of people in specific places. The conditions and trends indicated by groups of agents will at times find their way into our thought processes as external ideas. These are modes of thought generally made possible by computers, but they will deeply penetrate into episodes in our lives and shape the basis of our thinking.

We live in an era when the possibility of direct democracy through the Internet is seriously discussed. Architecture that gradually acquires qualities like complicated natural systems while adopting externalities accepts others (externalities), recalling the evolution of architecture that acquires a more advanced "ego" by discarding some sort of purity.

The design for the *Museum of Art & Library, Ota*[10] (2014-16, p. 248) was an experimental project in which joint discussions were held with residents, various experts, administrative staff and others, and important design decisions were made on the spot, with expectations for other-oriented thinking of the kind described above. There was a request to create a base to revive the flow of pedestrians in front of the station in a sedate provincial city. Above and beyond creating a museum and a library, it was important to design a diverse venue in which people with various backgrounds, ages, and orientations could find comfortable places, in other words to maximize "ecological niches" in a figurative sense. For that reason it was effective to incorporate many opinions, including those of actual potential users, into the design. In this way, a work of architecture that incorporated externality design ideas and was diversely eroded actually came to be crowded with numerous residents.

った。しかしその結果が正しいものなのかどうかを人間はトレースすることができない。そこで構造家は、FEM解析の結果を、人間が理解できるより単純なモデルによって検証した結果と照らし合わせる。仮説的理論と外部的思考の往復運動のような思考のもっとも基礎的な例だといえるかもしれない。

　ビッグデータやAIの時代において、同様の思考形態は、より高度に展開されるだろう。自分自身が構築した、理解可能な単純性を備えた思考と、非理論的計算過程とでもいうべき、他者的思考のブレンドを前提とした、新しい思考形態の可能性が示唆されている。この非理論的な計算過程には、現実の自然現象も含まれるだろうし、ある特定の空間特性に対する多数の人びとの反応とか、特定の場のなかでの人びとの多様な振る舞いといったものも含まれるだろう。エージェントの群れが示す様態とか傾向のようなものが、他者的な思考として、自分自身の思考のなかに時々に入り込むようにして考えること。これらは概ねコンピューターによって可能になった思考形態だが、私たちのものの考え方の根底、エピステーメーと呼べるようなものにまで深く浸透するだろう。

　私たちは、インターネットを介した直接民主制の可能性すら、真剣に議論される時代に生きている。外部性を取り入れながら次第に複雑な自然物のような質を獲得する建築——それは、〈他者〉を受け入れ、ある種の純粋さを捨てることによってより高度な「自我」を獲得する建築の進化を思わせる。

　太田市美術館・図書館[10] (2014-16, p. 248) の設計において、市民や各種専門家、行政の担当者らと同じ場を共有して議論し、その場で設計上の重要な選択を行うという実験的な試みを行った背景には、上記のような他者的思考への期待があった。地方都市の閑散とした駅前に歩く人の流れを甦らせる拠点をつくることが求められていた。美術館であり図書館であるということ以前に、さまざまなバックグラウンド、年齢層、指向性の人びとが、それぞれ自分の快適な場所を見つけることができるような、多様性を備えた場を設計することが必要だった。つまり、比喩的な意味での「生態学的ニッチ」を最大化すること。そのために文字通りの使い手を含む多数的思考を、設計に取り入れることが有効だった。このようにして設計思考の外部性を獲得し、多様に〈浸食〉された建築は、実際に多くの市民で賑うものとなっている。

[10] Museum of Art & Library, Ota (2014-16)

Process Record

When talking to a marine biologist, I was told that there are no purely formed jellyfish in the natural world. For example, a solmissus incisa[12] has regularly aligned protrusions on its circumference, but all of them are missing some. However, this lack is due to the process record of that individual, and these jellyfish are highly useful in marine biology research. While listening to this, I was thinking about giant trees[11]. A huge tree hundreds of years old does not appear pure, and its shape surely betrays some aspects of its life story, such as a scars from when it was struck by lightning. However, we are somehow strongly attracted to such impure forms. This is why the jellyfish illuminates something very simply: even if we are not biologists, we prefer the vestiges of time passing, as implied by imperfect shapes, to the timeless data conveyed by pure forms. And that is probably because accumulations of time, frozen on these cross-sectional surfaces, remind us of life itself.

A Medium to Record Events

Whatever pure geometric principle is used to create a building reflecting diverse conditions, as a "life form" it may suffer from some lack of information, as the jellyfish is always imperfect. Architecture that is truly alive must be engraved with some traces of time, but this is not true of architecture designed with pure algorithms. The latter is a timeless "perfect jellyfish" that is only a bundle of operations unrelated to time in terms of events unfolding.
I had an experience contrasting to this with the design of the *Home for All* in Rikuzentakata[13] (2011). The majority of the city was destroyed by the tsunami of 2011, and multiple architects collaborated to create a place where people forced to live in dull, dry temporary housing felt free to gather. This design arose from a process where various actual events overlapped just like a narrative. We joined local residents in going over, one by one, the qualities that this place ought to have. Cedar posts stood upright by the tsunami, silhouettes of houses, proportions resembling a turret, people gathering like a chain of small circles, a non-directionality resembling that of the mountain topography... Each characteristic emerged through interactions with the site each time we visited it. Here architecture served as a medium to record events.

Hierarchy: Jagged Diversity

The Rikuzentakata project might be a rare example of architecture taking on its original, primal role in what was in some sense an ideal state: a state of emergency in a disaster-stricken area. Architecture ought to be forged in the crucible of various ideas from people who create it, and then grow organically. However, the design of modern public buildings tends to be a process of architects merely translating programs designated by municipal authorities into building form.

[11] giant tree

履歴

　ある海洋生物学者と話したとき、自然界には純粋なかたちをしたクラゲはいない、と彼は言った。たとえばカッパクラゲ[12]は外周上に規則正しく並ぶ突起を持っているが、必ず何箇所か欠落しているのだという。しかしその欠落こそが、その個体の〈履歴〉を示す記録媒体であり、そのような欠落したクラゲによって海洋生物的研究が可能になるのだと。

　僕はそれを聞いて巨樹のことを想起していた。数百年の樹齢をもつ巨樹[11]は、純粋な姿をしておらず、落雷の跡など、必ず何らかの痕跡をその姿のうちに留めている。しかしその純粋でない姿に、私たちはむしろ強く惹かれる。その理由を、クラゲの話はとても単純に照らし出している。私たちは、生物の研究者でなくとも、純粋なかたちのもつ無時間的な情報よりも、不完全なかたちが暗示する時間の痕跡を好む。それは多分、そのような切断面として留められた時間の積み重ねこそが、生きていることそのものだからである。

出来事の記録媒体

　だとすれば、純粋な幾何学的原理のみを援用して、どれだけ多様な条件を反映した建築をつくっても、それは不完全なクラゲがもつような、生命としての情報量がないものになってしまうのかもしれない。

　本当の意味で生きている建築には、何らかの時間の痕跡が刻まれていなければならないのだが、純粋なアルゴリズムだけで設計された建築には、そのような特性がない。そこには出来事としての時間と結び付けられることのない、オペレーションの束があるだけであり、いわば無時間的な、「完全なクラゲ」なのである。

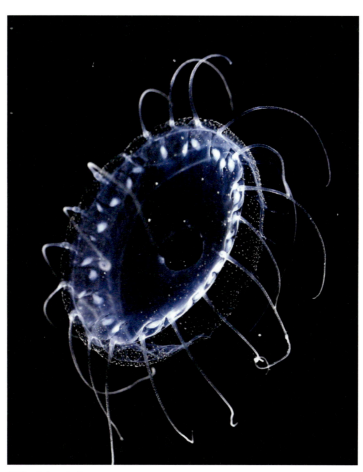

[12] solmissus incisa

The act of constructing a building can be a dynamic one, in which the latent ideas of various people and the actions involve in launching it intertwine, even if it does not quite equal the Rikuzentakata project.

Let us examine the wild hierarchical structure mentioned in section "Hierarchy (p. 024)" under a different light and in a different context. This model, in which architectural elements that are mutually other are intertwined hierarchically, can be interpreted as having a sort of temporality, as a chain of events that gradually deepens the degree of interaction hierarchically from higher to lower. Ota may be an example, in which a hierarchy, consisting of several boxes, the rim around them, and the architectural furnishings derived from it. In formulating a design in collaboration with residents and experts, matters were decided sequentially at meetings during the design period, with items on the agenda including the number of boxes, their arrangement, how to wind the rim around it, and the accompanying behaviors. This was to be engraved in the process record of the design, as an event that could not be reset or reproduced, shared with many participants. In fact, it was the concept of architecture having a "wild hierarchical structure" that made this possible. It was a jagged and diversified architecture, with faults between the elements of hierarchies (and thus open to interventions from other ways of thinking).

[13] Home for All in Rikuzentakata (2011)

陸前高田みんなの家[13]（2011）の設計においては、これと対照的な経験をした。津波で街の大部分を失い、無味乾燥な仮設住宅での日々を余儀なくされた人びとが、気軽に集えるような場所を、複数の建築家の協働でつくり上げた。この建築が生まれたプロセスは、まるで物語のように、ある具体的な出来事の重層として展開した。私たちは、現地の人びととともに、この場所にあるべきものの姿を、一つひとつ積み重ねていった。津波で立ち枯れた杉の丸太柱、家のようなシルエット、櫓のようなプロポーション、小さな輪が連鎖したような人びとの集まり方、山際の地形がもつ無方向的な感じ……。そういった具体的な特性がその都度、現地とのやり取りを通して浮かび上がっていった。建築は、いわばその出来事の記録媒体として建ち上がったのである。

〈階層〉——ギザギザとした多様性

陸前高田の例は被災地の非常事態、ある種の理想状態のなかで、建築というものが原初的に建ち上がった稀有な例なのかもしれない。建築とは、本来、それをつくり上げる人びとのさまざまな思いの坩堝のなかから、生えるように建ち上がるものだからだ。しかし現代の公共建築の設計は、自治体がつくった与件としてのプログラムを、建築家がある建築形式に翻訳するだけの作業になりがちである。

建築をつくるという出来事そのものが、さまざまな人びとの潜在的な思いと、それを建ち上げる設計行為がからみ合う、ダイナミックなものであり得る。陸前高田ほどではないにせよ。

「階層（p. 025）」の項で触れた、野性的な階層構造の話は、このような文脈のもとで、異なる光をもちはじめる。互いに〈他者〉であるような建築の要素が、階層的にからみ合うこのモデルは、ある種の時間性を内包したものとして解釈できるからだ。階層的に上位のものから下位のものへと、次第にからまりの度合いを深くしていく出来事の連鎖として。たとえば太田市美術館・図書館において、複数のボックス、その周りを巡るリム、それにからむ建築的家具といったもののなす〈階層〉は、まさにそのようなものだったのかもしれない。市民や専門家との協働設計において、ボックスの個数、配置、リムの巻き付け方、そこでの振る舞い、といった事項は、それぞれの会議で決定すべき議題として、設計期間のなかで順次確定していったからだ。それは、そこに参加する多数の人びとと共有した、二度と再現し得ない、リセットできない出来事として、設計のなかに〈履歴〉として刻まれることになったのである。逆にいうと、それを可能したのが、この野性的な階層構造をもった建築の考え方だったのだ。それは階層の要素と要素の間にある種の断層を伴った（それゆえに他者的な思考の介入を受け入れられる）、ギザギザとした多様性をもつ建築である。

This 12-story housing complex was built in Taipei. I wanted to design an apartment building that would be suitable for Taiwanese people, who have devised various intermediate areas in their daily lives to deal with the country's hot and humid climate, and would also have a 21st-century sensibility. So, rather than a standard floor plan, I opted for a setback form while trying to work around the building regulations in order to furnish each unit with a large terrace. The terraces are covered by a roof and trees, creating a comfortable and three-dimensional intermediate area on the surface of the building. A rigid-frame structure with a six-meter grid is covered with a roof-framing system with a three-meter grid. The roofs have a uniform pitch and different kinds of expressions can be made by altering the direction of the incline. The gradient distribution can be used to bifurcate the flow of rainwater or to form a network, and the roofs, gutters, and thin vertical columns create a rhythm on the building's surface. The wind that blows through the city is softly dispersed over the entire surface, making the terraces more comfortable, and minimizing the outbreak of "building wind." The work is a prototype for a high-rise building suited to 21st-century Asia in which the flow of water and air become entangled.

台北市に建つ地上12階建ての集合住宅である。高温多湿な気候とうまく付き合うさまざまな中間領域を、生活のなかで工夫してきた台湾の人びとにふさわしい、しかし同時に21世紀的な新しさをもった集合住宅は考えられないか。そこでわれわれは基準階平面のタワーではなく、斜線制限をかわしながらセットバックする形状を選択し、すべての住戸が大きなテラスをもてるようにした。テラスは屋根や樹木で覆われ、建物表面に立体的で快適な中間領域ができる。6mグリッドのラーメン構造を3mグリッドの屋根架構システムで覆っている。屋根の勾配は一定で、傾きの方向を変えることで変化のある表情をつくり出している。勾配方向の分布は、雨水の流れの分岐、あるいはネットワークをつくり、屋根、縦樋と細い鉛直柱が立面にリズムを与える。都市を流れる風は、凹凸の多い形状によって、表面全体に分散的にやわらかくいき渡り、テラスの快適性を高め、「ビル風」の発生を最小化することにもなる。水や空気の流れがからまる、21世紀のアジアにふさわしい高層建築のプロトタイプである。

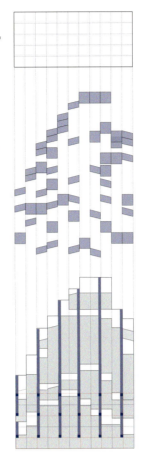

Systematic structure system on the 3000mm and 6000mm Grid.

PV roof on the 3000mm Grid

Consider the sunlight and drain system, roof direction is decided.

The three-meter-square, steel-framed roofs all have the same gradient, but changing the direction of the incline in each place causes rainwater to flow down the gutters evenly. The flow of rain becomes a facade.

3m角の平面をもつ鉄骨の屋根はどれも同じ傾きをもつが、場所ごとに傾きの方向を変え、雨水が均等に縦樋に流れ落ちる。水の流れがファサードになっている。

Colum on the 6000mm Grid

Reinforced-concrete structure base on 6000mm grid system.

Plan on the 3000mm Grid

To make the maximum volume, decide the plan by cutting the volume according to the regulation.

ASSEMBLY DIAGRAM

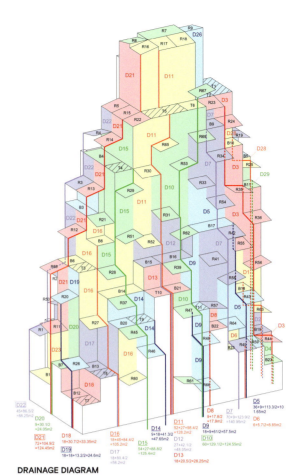

DRAINAGE DIAGRAM

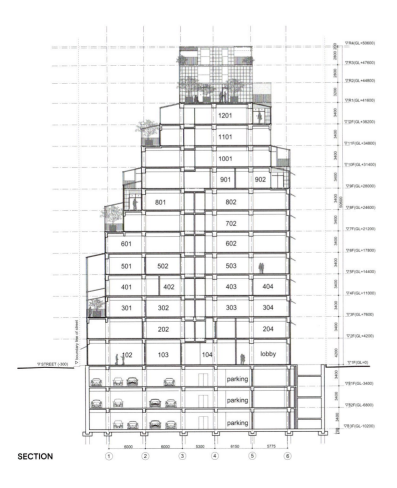

SECTION

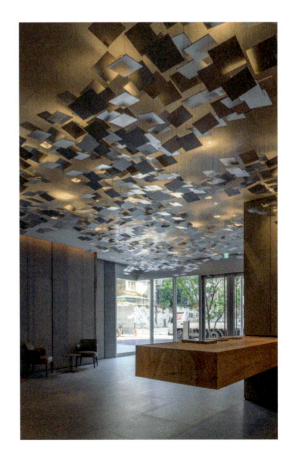

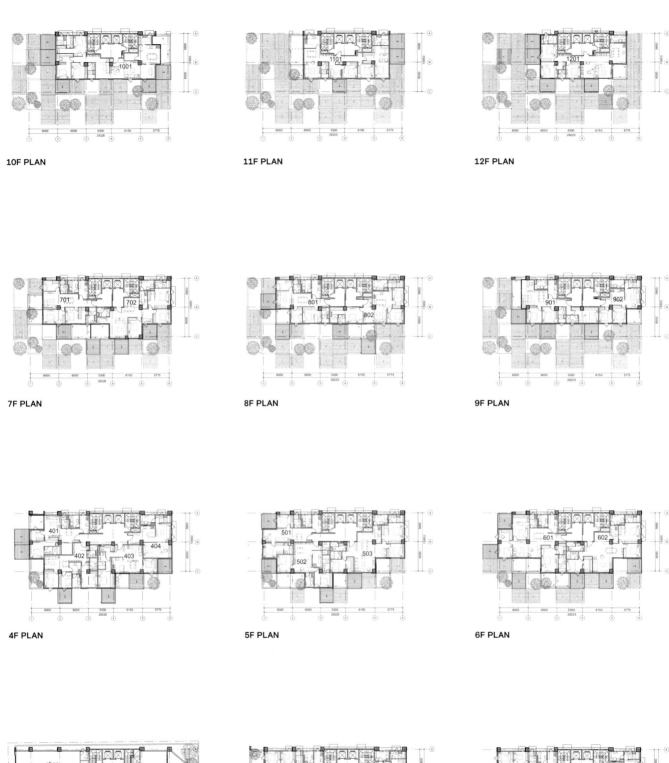

10F PLAN

11F PLAN

12F PLAN

7F PLAN

8F PLAN

9F PLAN

4F PLAN

5F PLAN

6F PLAN

1F PLAN

2F PLAN

3F PLAN

Taipei Roofs

Museum Forest of "Hill Valley"
台南市美術館 "丘谷之森"

2014-

This is a plan for an art museum in a historical district of Tainan, Taiwan. Tainan is home to many historical brick structures, such as castle walls and Fort Provintia, and the textuality of the soil used to make the bricks helps define the image of the city.With this context in mind, I devised a museum as an earthen transformational body in which the building and the ground are combined like a hill or valley protruding from the surface of the earth. The plan calls for the creation of a public garden, which can be used by local people, on the terrain, and the planting of trees to produce a continuum of leafy shade. The exhibit space, adjacent to the rooftop garden, will enable visitors to enjoy a variety of outdoor art, and it will also function as an open place that draws in natural light. The first floor contains educational area, which can be used for restaurants, shops, and workshops, and a storage area, which provides a glimpse of the museum collection, giving rise to a town-like place that people can pass through. This type of spatiality, consisting of a fluid interior space and a rooftop garden, where visitors can stroll freely, has parallels with Tainan's spontaneously generated streets. Thus, I consciously set out to create a connection with the existing network of streets. I intended the building to be an amalgam made up of a perfect harmony between natural and artificial elements – as if it had sprung up from the soil of Tainan.

台湾、台南市の歴史的街区に建てる美術館の提案である。台南は城壁や、赤嵌楼をはじめとするレンガを用いた歴史的建造物が多く、レンガの土のテクスチャリティが街の印象と結びついている。こういった文脈のなかに、台南の地表面から隆起した「丘」と「谷」のような、建物と地面が混在する土の変容体としての美術館を考えた。地形の上には地域の人も利用できる公共的な庭をつくり、樹木を植え、木陰の連続体をつくり出す。さまざまな屋外アートを楽しむことが可能となり、屋上庭園に隣接した展示スペースは、自然光を採り入れた開放的な場所となった。1階はレストラン、ショップ、ワークショップなどもできる教育エリア、コレクションの構成が垣間見える収蔵エリアなどであり、通り抜けできる街のような場所である。こうした流動的な内部空間、自由に散策できる屋上の庭のもつ空間性は、台南の自然発生的な街路に通じるものがあり、既存の街路ネットワークとの接続を意識している。台南の土から生えてきたような、自然と人工が渾然一体となったアマルガムとしての建物の成り立ちを意図した。

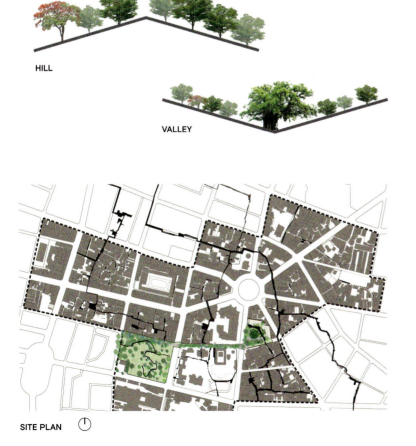

SITE PLAN

VALLEY

1F PLAN

2F PLAN

3F PLAN

4F PLAN

HILL

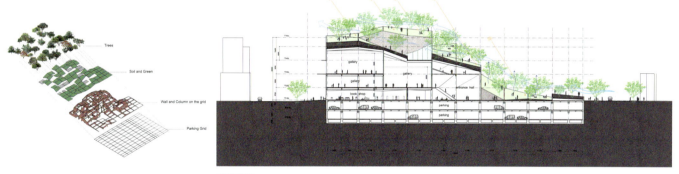
SECTION

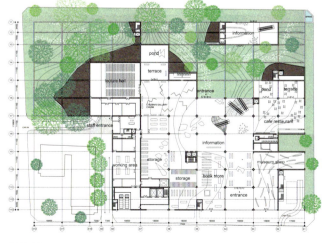
1F PLAN

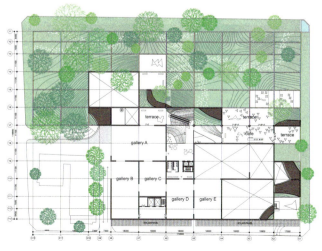
3F PLAN

Museum Forest of "Hill Valley"

Overlap House

2016-2018, Tokyo, Japan

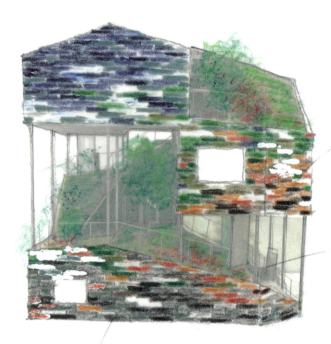

This is a proposal for a housing complex in Minami-Otsuka, Tokyo. Over time, a city adds new folds of history to an existing history, giving it a distinctive flavor. This is akin to the conditions of a life form, which incorporates and displays the history of evolution through its body. Instead of trying to erase the history of the city, I attempted to creatively turn it into multiple layers. To me, this seemed like a good way of increasing the degree of life there. In this project, I focused on the three formative layers of the city: the local terrain, houses with gardens, and materiality and color. The site abutted a relatively steep slope. This inspired me to make a building that would connect with the sloping road as an extension of the city's ground surface. By combining this with the given condition of designing a multiple dwelling complex consisting of three houses, I arrived at the idea of layering the houses (all equipped with a garden). In addition, I covered the roof and walls with a streaked slate pattern that seemed to mimic the nonchalant coloring of various elements in the surrounding town. By breathing life into the city's history, I created architecture that was both new and familiar.

東京都南大塚に建つ集合住宅の提案である。街は時間のなかで自らの履歴に新たな履歴を折り重ねて、独特の味わいを獲得する。それは、進化の履歴を身体に織り込みながら表出する、生命のありようと同じである。街の履歴を消すのではなく、創造的にそれを重層させること。それが街の生命の度合いを高めるのではないか。ここではこの街を形成している3つの層に着目した。すなわち、街の地形／庭付き一戸建て／マテリアリティーと色彩である。敷地は比較的急な坂に面している。そういう街の地表面の拡張として、坂道と連続する建築を考えた。そしてそれを、3軒の集合住宅をつくるという与件と重ねた時、3つの庭付き一戸建てを積層する、というアイデアに至った。加えて周辺の街の中にあるさまざまな要素の何気ない色合いを、擬態のように反映したスレートのまだらなパターンで屋根と壁を覆っている。街の履歴にさらなる生命を吹き込む、新しくも懐かしい建築である。

Overlap House

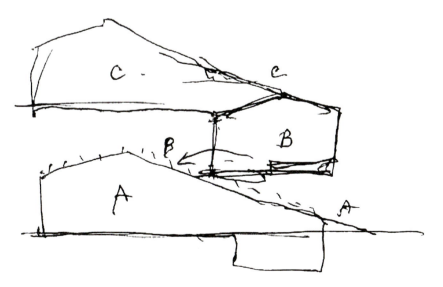

3F PLAN

2F PLAN

1F PLAN

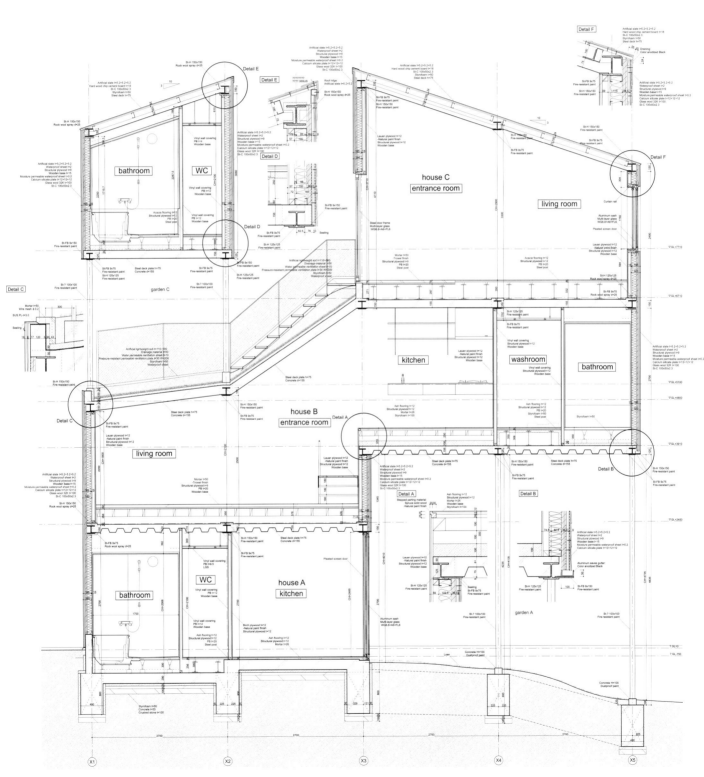

DETAILED SECTION

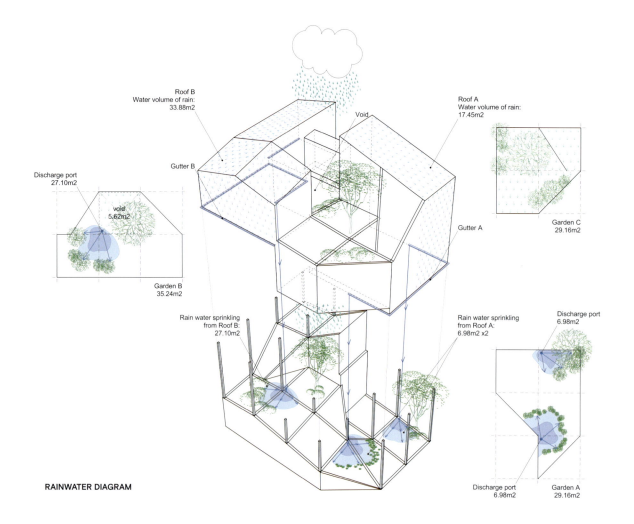

RAINWATER DIAGRAM

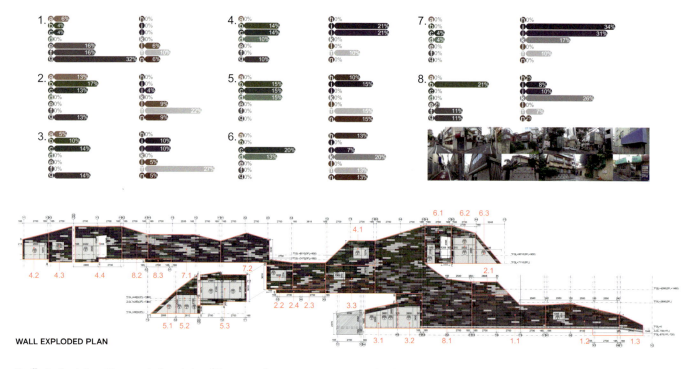

WALL EXPLODED PLAN

To effectively mimic and incorporate the coloring of the surrounding traditional shitamachi neighborhood, eight shades of readymade colonial slate were blended to make the elevation surface. Each color of slate was transported and cut on site, and a recipe was created to determine the blend ratio for each section of the wall. The actual lamination work was entrusted to craftsmen.

周辺の下町の色彩感を擬態的に取り入れるために、8色のコロニアル・スレートの既製品をブレンドした立面としている。スレートは色ごとに現場にカートで搬入し、壁の部位ごとにブレンドの割合のみを指定したレシピをつくり、実際の貼り込みは職人の手に委ねて施行する。

Overlap House

Overlap House

Sarugaku

2006–2007, Tokyo, Japan

This aggregation of buildings for commercial tenants was built in the Daikanyama district of Tokyo. Legal restrictions made it necessary to create multiple buildings, approximately the size of houses, on the relatively small site, so we opted for several mountain-like stepped volumes. This approach produced valley-like spaces between the "mountains," which I hoped to fill up with people and displays of products. While shops that abut regular streets are widened in regard to the street, here it was possible to widen the shops on every floor of the buildings. The openings were made with a vertical aspect that continues across the various levels, but depending on the viewing angle, the depth of the levels changes, making it appear to be alternatively connected or detached. The openings were also designed to create a link between the volumes. Instead of a building that attempts to eliminate things and people, I strove to make a building with a sense of vitality that would grow stronger when it brimmed with these elements. In this way, the shopping space promises to be a kind of natural environment for hunting and gathering that taps into our wild instincts.

東京、代官山に建つ商業テナントビルの集合体である。法的な条件から、比較的狭小な敷地にほぼ住宅規模の店舗ビルを複数建てることが要求されたが、私たちは「山」のような段状のボリュームを複数置くことにした。それによって「山」の間にできた「谷」状のスペースが、人びとやディスプレイされた物たちであふれることを意図したのである。通常街路に面した店舗は、道に対して店を広げているが、ここでは各層で店を広げることが可能である。開口は段にまたがって連続するように縦長に開けられるが、段の奥行きによって見る角度が変わるとつながったり離れたりする。開口はまた、ボリューム相互をまたいで連続するように計画されている。ものや人を排除するような建築ではなく、それらがあふれることによって強さを獲得するような、生命感のある建築をつくることを目指した。それによって、買い物をする空間は狩猟採集をする自然環境のような人間の野生に開かれたものになるだろう。

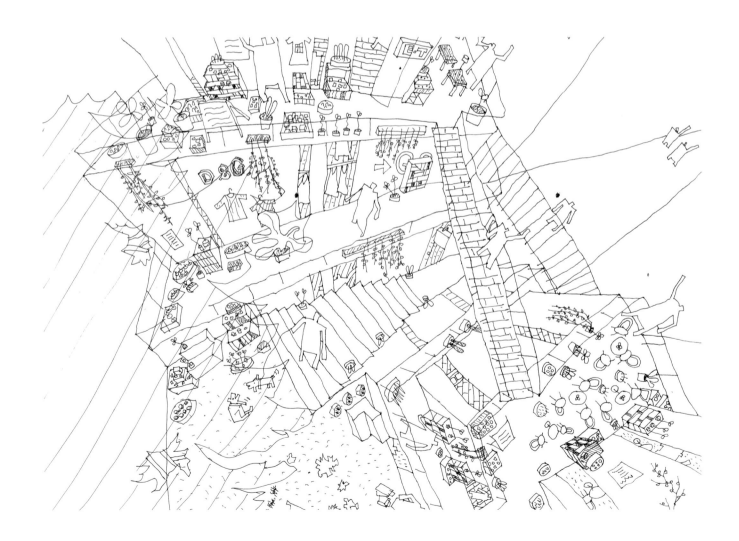

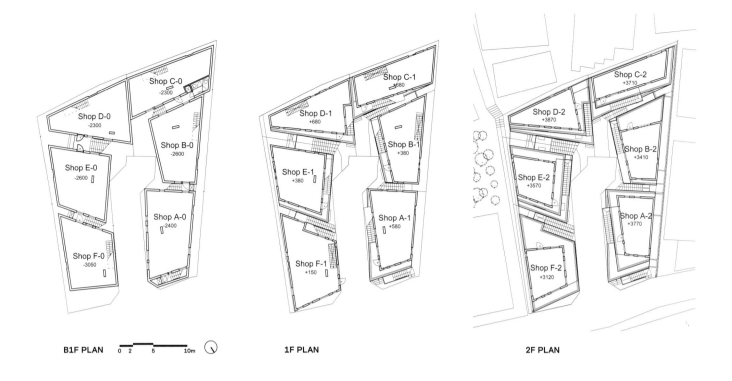

B1F PLAN 0 2 5 10m

1F PLAN

2F PLAN

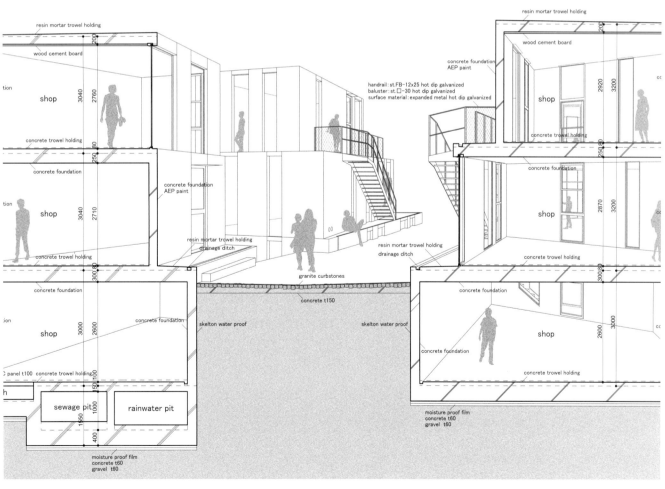

SECTION

Sarugaku

Sarugaku

Art Museum & Library, Ota
太田市美術館・図書館

2014-2016, Gunma, Japan

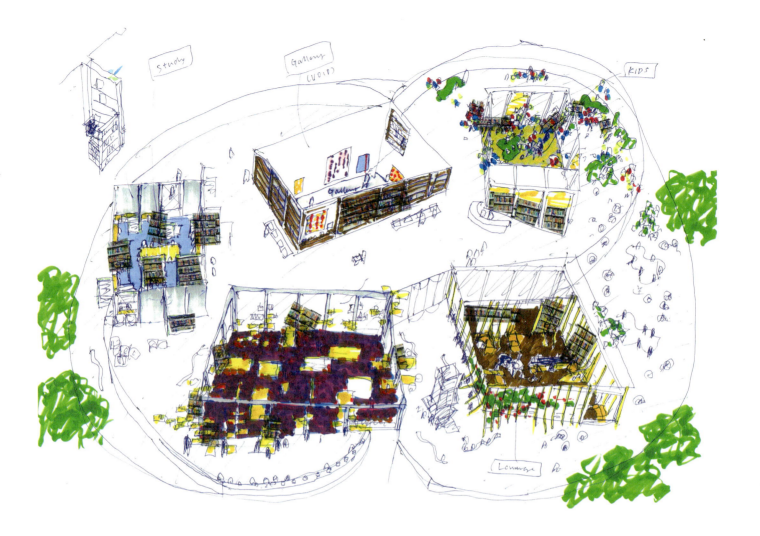

This cultural exchange facility was built in front of Ota Station in Gunma Prefecture. One aim of the project was to create a base that would draw a stream of people back to the front of the station, which had become largely deserted. Another aim was to create something that would make a connection between the town and the building's interior, encouraging people to casually drop by. It was also necessary to create a place that was wholly unique to Ota. Using the image of a wing and propeller, a reference to the Nakajima Aircraft Company, which had once operated in the city, I attempted to evoke a state in which the building would serve as a node for multiple streams. In concrete terms, I proposed a structure in which a slope would wind around and around five reinforced-concrete boxes by means of a steel rim. This enables people to naturally make their way to every floor as if they were walking through the city. In addition, I tried to create a three-dimensional symbiosis of places with a diverse range of characteristics to enable people of many different ages and backgrounds to discover their own place. The book shelves and works of art are visible through the window, making people want to go inside, and in the same way that a museum or a library exudes a welcoming air by providing us with a glimpse of its contents, the building precipitates a stream of people. Designed to entangle a large number of local residents and staff, the building is like a flower that was born in front of the station.

群馬県太田駅前に建つ、文化交流施設である。閑散とした駅前に人の流れを取り戻すための拠点をつくることが、建設の目的であり、人びとが気軽に立ち寄れるように、街が内部まで連続しているような建築を目指した。また、他のどこでもない太田だけの場所にする必要もあった。かつてこの街にあった中島飛行機の、翼やプロペラのイメージから、複数の流れの結び目のような建築のありようが喚起された。具体的には5つのRC造の「ボックス」の周りに、鉄骨造の「リム」によるスロープがぐるぐると取り巻く構成を提案した。人は街を歩くように、自然に各階を巡ることができる。また、さまざまな年齢層やバックグラウンドの人びとが、それぞれ自分の場所を見つけられるように、多様な特性をもった場所を立体的に共存させようとした。外部からはガラスを通して内部の本棚やアートが見え、中に入りたくなる雰囲気をつくり、美術館や図書館からもお互いが垣間見えることで、人の流れを誘発している。多数の市民や関係者を巻き込みつつ設計され、駅前に生まれた花のような建築である。

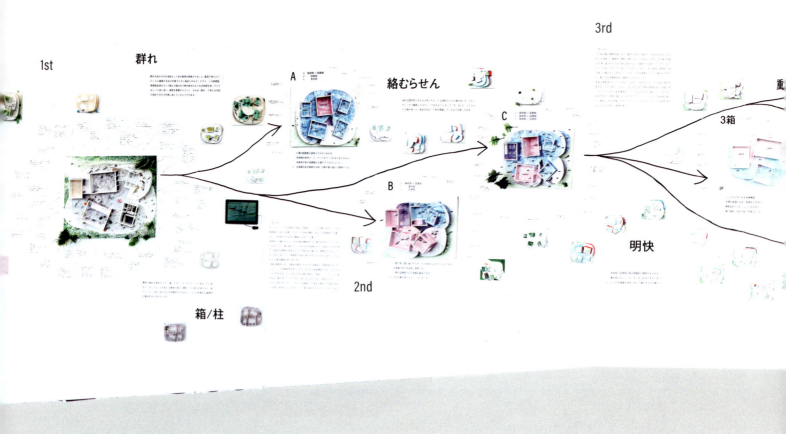
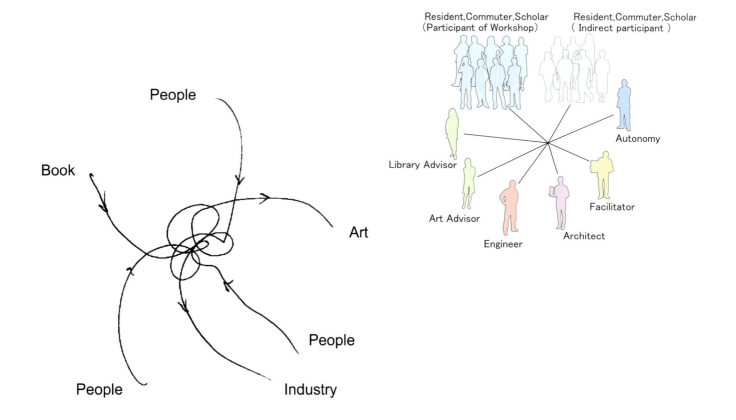

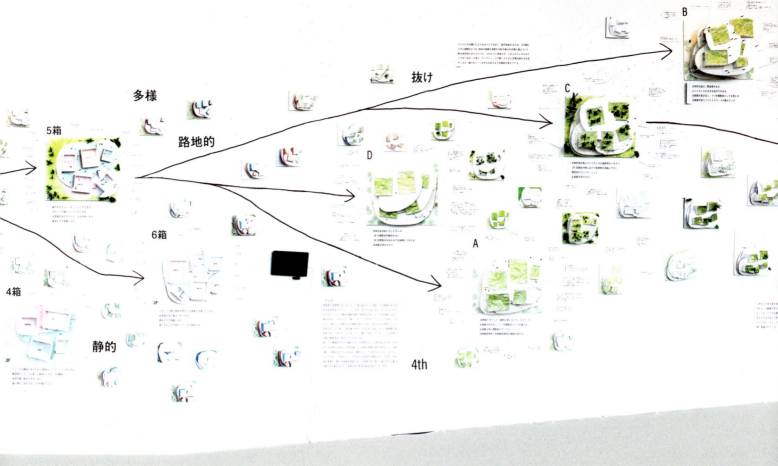

This project was intended to create a base that would bring the flow of walking people back to the front of the station. The design process was presented in a discussion forum with the public and evolved in a natural manner. Important decisions about the characteristics we wanted to include in the project were made at a series of discussions. A clear theme was established for each meeting (branding libraries and museums, a number of individual boxes, making a winding slope, etc.) and after presenting several possible plans for each theme, participants discussed and selected the one they preferred. The first half of the meetings was devoted to a kind of lecture in which a basic explanation of each theme was presented with the help of models that were intelligible to anyone, regardless of their background. As a result, the discussion and selection process conducted in the second half led to some very interesting structures. The architectural proposal also evolved from a clean plan involving saplings to a wilder plan with giant trees, which even included some impure elements. This experience conveyed the fact making architecture can be a bundle of irreversible events shared by many people while also suggesting that architecture itself has the ability to function as a recording medium for events.

駅前に歩く人の流れを取り戻す拠点をつくること。そのデザインプロセスを市民との議論の場に開くことは、自然な流れだった。私たちの取り組みの特徴は、議論の場で重要なデザイン上の決定を行なったことである。毎回明確なテーマを決め（図書館と美術館のブランドの仕方／箱の個数／スロープの巻きつけ方など）、それぞれに対しあり得る複数の検討案を作成し、選択を協議した。セッションの前半はレクチャー形式でテーマのバックボーンを説明し、専門家でなくても理解できるように各案の模型を用意した。結果、後半の議論と選択は興味深く建設的なものとなった。建築案もプロポーザル当初のクリーンな若木のような案から、不純さすら孕んだ巨樹のように野生的な案に変容した。それは、建築をつくることが多数の人びとと共有された不可逆的な出来事の束となる経験であり、建築そのものが出来事の記録媒体としての姿にもなり得ることを示唆している。

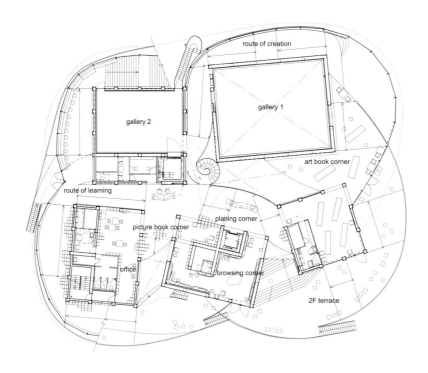

2F PLAN

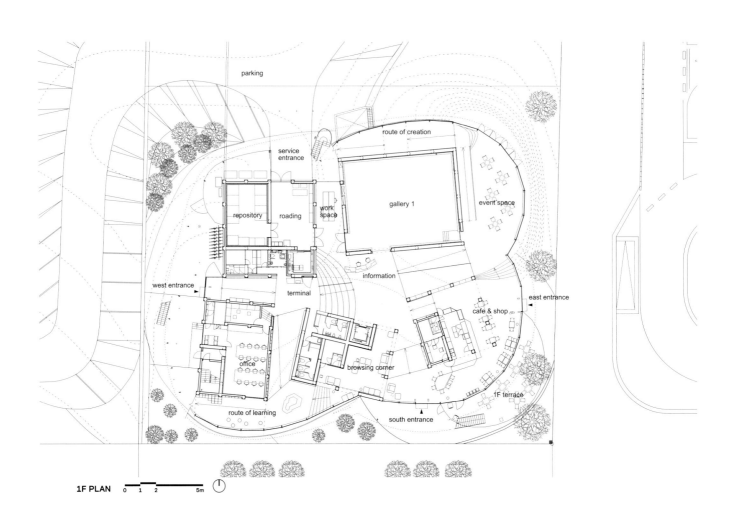

1F PLAN 0 1 2 5m

RF PLAN

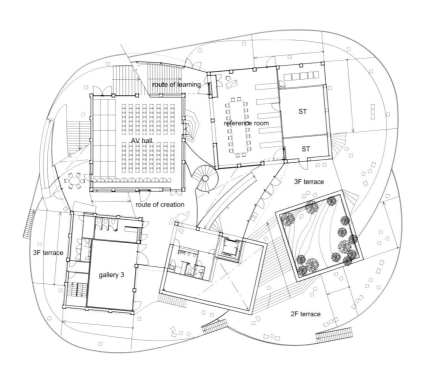

3F PLAN

Structuring the rims out of steel-framed joists and a synthetic deck, and installing a rigid, reinforced concrete core with ample planar balance moderated the effect of the horizontal brace created by the sloping form of the rims' peripheries. Although the building's structure was made to be as simple as possible, a large number of tests related to the manner of use and other details were conducted to realize the attractive structural design.

リムは鉄骨小梁＋合成デッキで構成され、強固なRCコアを平面的にバランスよく設けることで、外周リムのスロープ形状からくる水平ブレース効果を和らげている。建物の構成は可能な限りシンプルな構成となっているが、その使い方や納まり方については現場においても多くの検証を行い、魅せる構造計画を実現している。

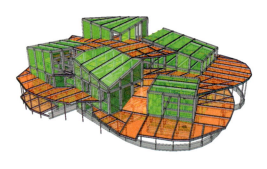

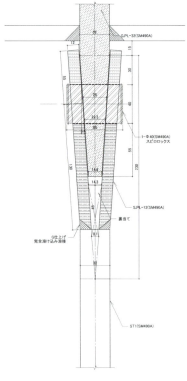

Atrium columns suspended from both ends
吹き抜け吊り柱頭脚両端部

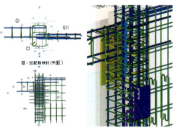

The connection between the bar arrangement in the box section and the steel-framed gusset plates
BOX部の配筋と鉄骨ガセットプレートの取り合い

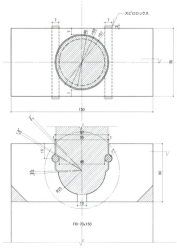

Head section of pin-type facade column
ファサードピン柱の柱頭部

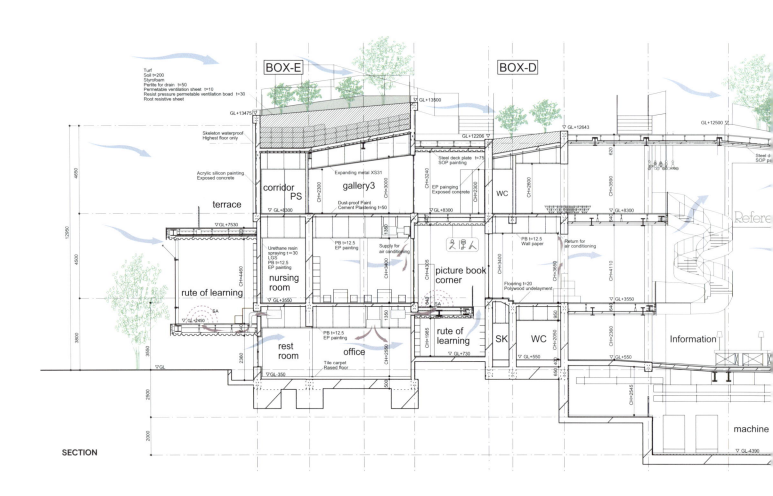

SECTION

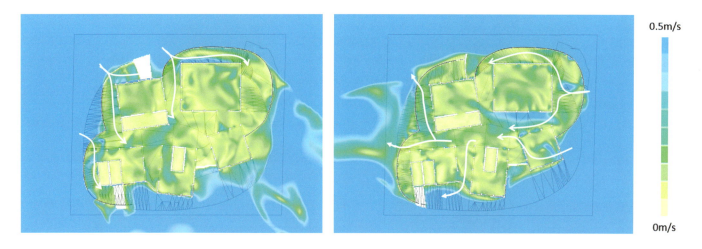

Outside air is introduced via a ventilator that deftly captures the prevailing wind (northwest to east) during an intermediary period. It flows gently (app. 0.1–0.2m/s) between a rim (laid out to encourage tangling) and a dispersion of boxes, improving ventilation in the building. The natural lighting plan, designed to create brightness based on the flow of air and the individual character of each space, was an important element in designing the rim and boxes.

主に中間期の卓越風(北西風〜東風)を上手に捉える換気窓から取り込まれた外気は、からまるようにレイアウトされたリムや分散するボックスの間を通って穏やかに流れ(0.1〜0.2m/s程度)、館内の通風を促す。こうした空気の流れや、空間ごとの個性に応じた明るさを目指した自然採光計画は、リムやボックスをデザインするための重要な要素となった。

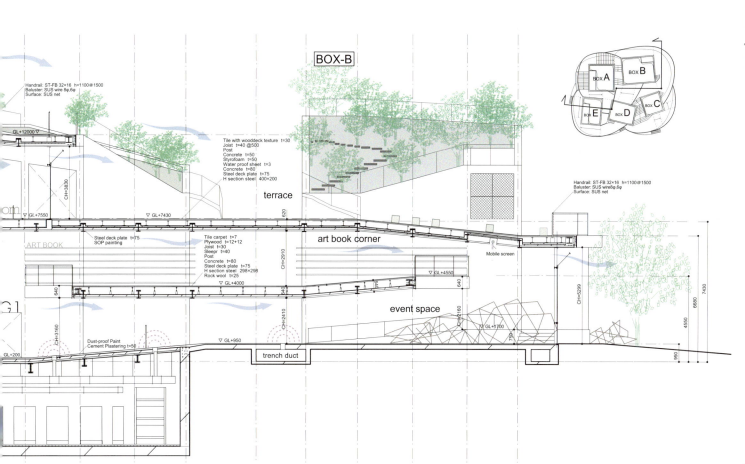

Art Museum & Library, Ota

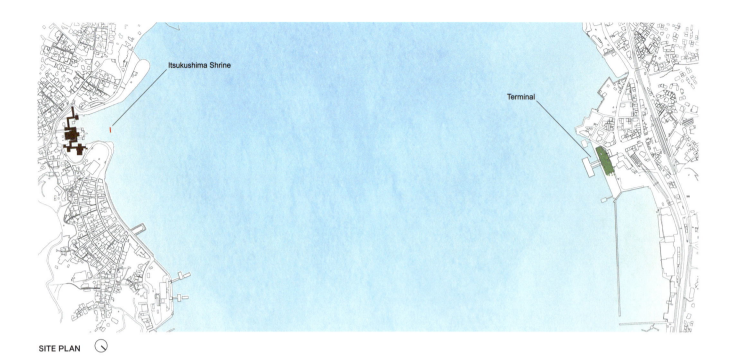

SITE PLAN

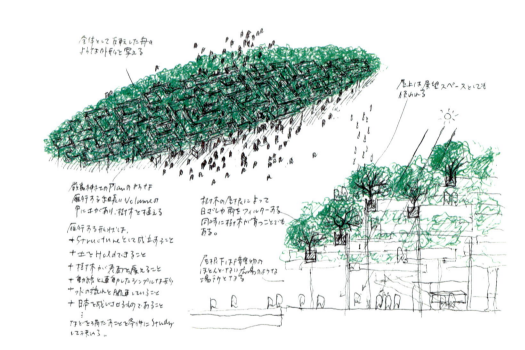

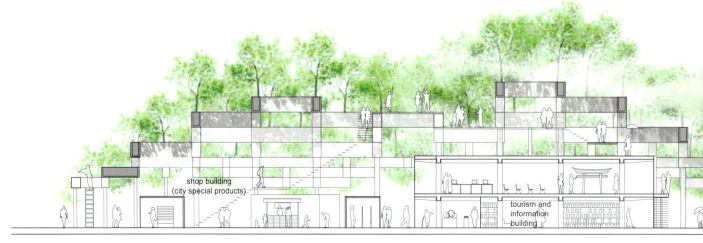

SECTION

This is a proposal for a ferry terminal on the island of Miyajima in Hiroshima Prefecture. I conceived of a place with budding greenery that would resemble a "floating island" formed by the trees stretching up into the air and also reflect the mystical atmosphere of Miyajima. Using a framework that recalled the ridge beams and large torii gate at Itsukushima Shrine (located on Miyajima), I arranged a group of freestanding, reinforced-concrete columns in a five-meter grid, and opted for a free structural system made from a hybrid of wood and steel. The truss, which contains planting soil, is specially designed to withstand dirt, rainwater, and sea breezes, creating a place that seems to be beneath a huge tree with sunlight filtering through the leaves. By installing a row of boxes housing things like shops and a visitor information center, which seem to have drifted in from the city, and temporary stands, the large, windswept terminal space, generates a bustle of activity, attracting a free flow of people that links the town and the sea. In this project, I set out to make a symbolic place, where on the one hand, tourists could sense the vitality of Miyajima, and on the other, local residents could meet in the midst of various day-to-day activities.

広島県宮島に建つフェリーターミナルの提案である。空中で成長する樹木がかたちづくる「うきしま」のようでありながら、宮島のもつ神秘的な空気感を反映した緑が芽吹く場所を考えた。厳島神社の棟木や大鳥居にも通じる架構として、5mグリッドで建ち上がるRC造の独立柱群を配置し、木と鉄のハイブリッドによる自由な構造システムを採用した。植栽土壌を内包する梁材は、土壌や雨水、海からの潮風などへの耐久性に十分配慮した仕様とし、木漏れ日が降り注ぐ巨樹の下のような場所をつくり出す。風の吹き抜ける大らかなターミナル空間は、街から流れ込んできたような店舗や観光案内の箱、仮設の屋台などが建ち並ぶことで、街と海をつなぐ自由な人の流れを誘発し、にぎわいをつくり出す。観光客が宮島の活力に触れる一方で、地元の人びとは日常を彩るさまざまなきっかけに出合うような、シンボリックな場所をつくることを意図した。

Afterword: Toward the Intelligence of the Jungle

The first thing I wanted to address fully was the soft regionalism that I tried to capture with the term tangle tab, with the words side, pleats, and lines shaping the discussion. This was because I thought this was where the foundations lay for coexistence of heterogeneous things, mediated by complex gradations of space and are not clearly separated.

Another important point is that the living world has a wild hierarchical structure. There is potential for architecture where diverse, heterogeneous things encounter and entangle with one another.

This leads us to the question of whether, beyond the issue of architectural form, it is possible to create living architecture with a high degree of life. When doing so, architecture will related to a mode of perception that we can call animalistic. Beyond that, we will see the emergence of intelligence that thinks in terms of gradation of space rather than by linguistic segment. This architecture as "new nature" is not only a process determined by a single architect in advance, but also incorporates the order of emergence and incorporates processes such as fermentation and erosion into the design.

In such cases, the design process involves various others and there are aspects that emerge through others' occurrences rather than being intended from the start. It is possible that organic life has acquired a more sophisticated manner by incorporating others, and that architecture is engraved in architecture as a certain kind of process record. In this case, wild hierarchical structures as the hierarchical structures of process record. These occurrences create a horizon where architecture itself becomes a social commitment.

 "New forms" and "new nature" have emerged in exchange for "departure from the human," by putting the meanings, customs and social possibilities created by humans in (parentheses). However, if human social activity remains part of the biological world, the new architectural approach arrived at through "departure from the human" may mean "encountering the human" again. This kind of "new commitment" connects to issues derived from human living conditions such as earth and to universal and unavoidably local issues such as pan locality.

We are aiming for architecture that conveys a variety of degrees of life, from the fluctuations at the dawn of the universe to the galaxies, microorganisms, higher organisms and even human culture, but can be widely interpreted in terms of the living world. This may entail an enormous number of diverse objects coming together and intertwining, forming an aggregate body with so many fault lines that it cannot be seen as a whole.

We may be approaching a new mode of intelligence that extends throughout the jungle, and moving towards a new order that is unquestionably architectural.

あとがき：ジャングルの知性へ

　〈からまりしろ〉という言葉で捉えようとしたふわふわとした領域性を、〈側〉〈ひだ〉〈ライン〉という言葉でかたちの問題として、まずはきちんと取り上げたかった。空間の複雑なグラデーションによって媒介される、はっきりと区切るのではない異質なものの共存の基礎が、そこにあると思っているからだ。

　生きている世界が野性的な〈階層〉構造をなしていることも重要である。互いに異質な、他者的な事物が、階層的に出合い、からまるような建築があり得るからである。

　それは、建築形式の問題を超えて、〈生の度合〉の高い、文字通り生きている建築というものが可能か、という問いへと私たちを導く。その時建築は、〈動物的〉ともいえるような知覚のありようと関係してくるだろう。その先に、言語的な分節によって思考する方法とは異なる、空間のグラデーションによって思考する知性が浮かび上がる。そのような「新しい自然」としての建築は、ひとりの建築家のあらかじめ意図した方法だけでなく、〈創発〉する秩序を取り入れたり、〈発酵・浸食〉といった過程を設計のなかに取り入れることによってより豊かに展開できるだろう。

　してみると、そのような設計過程には、さまざまな〈他者〉を巻き込み、最初から意図するというよりは、他者的な出来事のなかで浮かび上がる側面もあることになる。生命が〈他者〉を取り込むことによってより高度な様態を獲得したように、である。建築をつくることそのものが、ある〈履歴〉として建築に刻まれるような建築があり得る。その時野性的な階層構造は、そのまま〈履歴〉の階層構造としても解釈可能である。そのような出来事によって、建築をつくることそのものが社会的なコミットメントとなる地平が現出する。

　「新しいかたち」や「新しい自然」は、人間がつくり上げてきた意味や慣習や社会のありようを括弧に入れ、「人間から離れる」ことと引き換えに見出された。しかし、人間の社会的営みが、生きている世界の一部であることに変わりないとしたら、一旦「人間から離れる」ことによって獲得された新しい建築のアプローチは、再び「人間と出合う」ことができるのではないだろうか。このような「新しいコミットメント」は、〈土〉のように人の生きる条件から派生した意味性の問題や、〈汎ローカリティー〉のように私たちが避けることのできないローカリティーと普遍性のあいだにある問題とつながっていくだろう。

　私たちは、宇宙のはじまりのゆらぎから星雲、微生物、高等生物、ひいては人間の文化に至る、さまざまな〈生の度合〉をもった、しかし確実に生きている世界を、広く捉えられるような建築を目指している。それはおびただしい数の異質なものがからまり合い、ひとつの統合体に見えないくらいさまざまな断層を伴った多様体になるのかもしれない。

　私たちはもしかしたら、ジャングルに行き渡っているような知性のあり方に、近づいていくのかもしれない。確実に建築と呼べる新しい秩序に向かって。

Project Data

Taipei Complex
location: unbuilt / Taipei, Taiwan
principal use: composite facility (museum, shops, and restaurants)
scale: 7 stories, 3 basements
structure: reinforced concrete, steel frame
site space: 3,806.04m²
total floor space: 27,000m²
design period: 2015.4-
construction period: -
constructor: -
collaborative design: EnHance architects & associates

Foam Form
location: unbuilt / Takao, Taiwan
principal use: composite facility (bridge, theatre, office, and museum)
scale: 4 stories, 1 basement
structure: steel frame
site area: 71,340m²
total floor space: 70,900m²
design period: 2010.6-2011.1
construction period: -
constructor: -
collaborative design: Ricky Liu & Associate (collaborative design), Masato Araya / Oak Structural Design Office (structure), ARUP JAPAN (structure / equipment)

Coil
location: Tokyo, Japan
principal use: house
scale: 3 stories
structure: wood frame
site area: 35m²
total floor space: 108.00m²
design period: 2010.7-2011.7
construction period: -2011.8-2011.11
constructor: Ohara koumusho
collaborative design: tmsd Manda Takashi Structural Design Office (structure), Youko Ando Design (curtain), Izumi Okayasu (lighting)

Kamaishi City Disaster Recovery Public Housing
Kamaishi Nursery School
location: unbuilt / Iwate, Japan
principal use: residential complex / nursery school, kindergarden
scale:
    residential complex: 4 stories
    nursery school: 1 story, 1 basement
structure:
    residential complex: reinforced concrete, steel frame
    nursery school: wood frame, reinforced concrete
site area: nursery school: 871.m²
total floor space: 2,984.87m²
design period: 2013.1-2014.1
construction period: -
constructor: Daiwa Housing Industry Co., Ltd.
collaborative design:
    residential complex: ARUP JAPAN (structure / equipment)
    ARUP JAPAN (structure / equipment), Youko Ando Design (textiles)

Gallery S
location: unbuilt
principal use: gallery
scale: 5 stories
structure: steel frame, reinforced concrete
site area: -
total floor space: 207.90m²
design period: 2007.5-
construction period: -
constructor: -
collaborative design: Masato Araya / Oak Structural Design Office (structure)

Architecture Farm
location: unbuilt / Aodi, Taiwan
principal use: house
scale: 3 stories
structure: steel frame, reinforced concrete
site area: 253m²
total floor space: 495.00m²
design period: 2007.11-2008.6
construction period: -
constructor: -
collaborative design: -

Tree-ness House
location: Tokyo, Japan
principal use: gallery, residential complex
scale: 5 stories
structure: reinforced concrete
site area: 139.6m²
total floor space: 450m²
design period: 2009.1-2015.2
construction period: 2015.3-2017.7
constructor: Ohara komusho
collaborative design: Masato Araya / Oak Structural Design Office (structure), tmsd Manda Takashi Structural Design Office (structure), EOS Plus (equipment), Yuichi Tsukada (planting), Youko Ando Design (textiles)

Alp
location: Tokyo, Japan
principal use: residential complex
scale: 3 stories, 1 basement
structure: reinforced concrete
site area: 168.57m²
total floor space: 490.90m²
design period: 2008.2-2009.6
construction period: 2009.7-2010.3
constructor: Miura komuten
collaborative design: tmsd Manda Takashi Structural Design Office (structure), EOS plus (equipment), comodo setsubi keikaku

House of House
location: Kanagawa, Japan
principal use: information center
scale: 2 stories
structure: wood frame
site area: -
total floor space: 123.49m²
design period: 2006.9-2008.5
construction period: 2008.7-2008.8
constructor: Ao
collaborative design: Fontage (detail design, management), design / kozo kenkyusho (structure)

One-roof Apartment
location: Niigata, Japan
principal use: residential complex
scale: 4 stories
structure: reinforced concrete
site area: 300.46 m²
total floor space: 958.24m²
design period: 2007.10-2008.8
construction period: 2008.9-2010.3
constructor: Kubota kensetsu
collaborative design: Yoshihiko Yoshihara (collaborative design), Masato Araya / Oak Structural Design Office (structure), Akeno Facility Resilience Inc. (equipment)

Higashi-Totsuka Church
location: Kanagawa, Japan
principal use: church
scale: 2 stories
structure: steel frame
site area: 85.25 m²
total floor space: 114.57m²
design period: 2012.9-2013.11
construction period: 2013.12-2015.1
constructor: Ohara komusho
collaborative design: ARUP JAPAN (structure), Izuimi Okayasu (lighting)

House H
location: unbuilt
principal use: house
scale: 2 stories
structure: reinforced concrete
site area: -
total floor space: 82.1m²
design period: 2004.4-
construction period: -
constructor: -
collaborative design: tmsd Manda Takashi Structural Design Office(structure)

Masuya
location: Niigata, Japan
principal use: showroom and office
scale: 2 stories
structure: reinforced concrete
site area: 212.5m²
total floor space: 294.2m²
design period: 2005.5-2005.11
construction period: 2006.4-2006.9
constructor: Kubota kensetsu
collaborative design: tmsd Manda Takashi Structural Design Office (structure), ES Associates (equipment)

Bloomberg Pavilion
location: Tokyo, Japan
principal use: pavilion
scale: 1 story
structure: steel frame
site area: -
total floor space: 24.5m²
design period: 2010.5-2011.4
construction period: 2011.5-2011.10
constructor: Morikawa kensetsu, Kawano tekkotsu kogyo
collaborative design: Masato Araya / Oak Structural Design Office (structure / management)

Photosynthesis
location: Milan, Italy
principal use: installation
scale: -
structure: polycarbonate
site area: -
total floor space: 1,000m²
design period: 2010.10-2011.2
construction period: 2011.2-2011.4
constructor: NOMURA Co., Ltd., Xilografia
collaborative design: ARUP (structure)

Long House
location: unbuilt / Ochoalcubo, Chile
principal use: house
scale: 1 story
structure: reinforced concrete, steel frame
site area: -
total floor space: 200m²
design period: 2011.9-
construction period: -
constructor: -
collaborative design: Mitsuhiro Kanada (structure)

9hours Project
  9hours Akasaka
  9hours Takebashi
  9hours Asakusa
  9hours Shin-Osaka
  9hours Hamamatsucho
location: Tokyo and Osaka, Japan
principal use: lodging facility
scale:
  Akasaka: 4 stories, 1 basement
  Takebashi: 8 stories
  Asakusa: 9 stories
  Shin-Osaka: 8 stories
  Hamamatsucho: 10 stories
structure:
  Akasaka: steel frame, reinforced concrete
  Takebashi: steel frame
  Asakusa: steel frame
  Shin-Osaka: steel frame
  Hamamatsucho: steel frame
site area:
  Akasaka: 227.32m²
  Takebashi: 166.35m²
  Asakusa: 206.15m²
  Shin-Osaka: 233.59m²
  Hamamatsucho: 262.69m²
total floor space:
  Akasaka: 999.21m²
  Takebashi: 829.82m²
  Asakusa: 1,186.96m²
  Shin-Osaka: 989.41m²
  Hamamatsucho: 1,391.84m²
design period:
  Akasaka: 2016.2-2017.3
  Takebashi: 2016.8-2017.6
  Asakusa: 2016.10-2017.9
  Shin-Osaka: 2017.4-2017.10
  Hamamatsucho: 2017.4-
construction period:
  Akasaka: 2017.4-2018.4
  Takebashi: 2017.6-2018.3
  Asakusa: 2017.10-2018.8 (expected)
  Shin-Osaka: 2017.11-2018.9 (expected)
  Hamamatsucho: -
constructor:
  Akasaka: Shin Nihon kensetsu
  Takebashi: Daiho kensetsu
  Asakusa: Tsuboi kogyo
  Shin-Osaka: Daiwa Housing Industry Co., Ltd.
  Hamamatsucho: Shimizu Corporation
  collaborative design: EnHance architects & associates
collaborative design:
  Akasaka: tmsd Manda Takashi Structural Design Office (structure), EOS plus (equipment), Yuuichi Tsukada (planting), Masaaki Hiromura / Hiromura Design Office (signs), Fumie Shibata / Design Studio S (capsules, fixtures)
  Takebashi: TECTONICA INC. (structure), EOS plus (equipment), Masaaki Hiromura / Hiromura Design Office (signs), Fumie Shibata / Design Studio S (capsules, fixtures), SI Associates Co., Ltd. (sanitary facilities)
  Asakusa: TECTONICA INC. (structure), EOS plus (equipment), Masaaki Hiromura / Hiromura Design Office (signs), Fumie Shibata / Design Studio S (capsules, fixtures), GN setsubi keikaku (sanitary facilities)
  Shin-Osaka: Daiwa Housing Industry Co., Ltd. (detail design), Masaaki Hiromura / Hiromura Design Office (signs), ZYCC (furnitures), Fumie Shibata / Design Studio S (capsules, fixtures)
  Hamamatsucho: Shimizu Corporation (detail design), Masaaki Hiromura / Hiromura Design Office (signs), Fumie Shibata / Design Studio S (capsules, fixtures)

Taipei Roofs
location: Taipei, Taiwan
principal use: commercial facility, residential complex
scale: 15 stories, 3 basements
structure: reinforced concrete, steel frame
site area: 470m²
total floor space: 3,364m²
design period: 2013.2-2014.3
construction period: 2014.4-2018 (expected)
constructor: PAUIYAN archiland
collaborative design: PAUIYAN archiland, Cang Yu architecture office, Envision Engineering Consultants

Museum Forest of "Hill Valley"
location: unbuilt / Tainan, Taiwan
principal use: gallery
scale: 4 stories, 2 basements
structure: reinforced concrete
site area: -
total floor space: 26,636m²
design period: 2014.6-2014.9
construction period: -
constructor: -
collaborative design: Kenjiro Hosaka, MAYU architect

Overlap House
location: Tokyo, Japan
principal use: residential complex
scale: 3 stories
structure: steel frame
site area: 87.90m²
total floor space: 177.50m²
design period: 2016.5-2017.6
construction period: 2017.7-2018.5 (expected)
constructor: Ohara komusho
collaborative design: Masato Araya / Oak Structural Design Office (structure), EOS Plus (equipment), Yuuichi Tsukada (planting)

Sarugaku
location: Tokyo, Japan
principal use: commercial facility
scale: 2 stories, 1 basement
structure: reinforced concrete
site area: 299.3m²
total floor space: 851.46m²
design period: 2006.3-2007.1
construction period: 2007.2-2007.10
constructor: Matsushita sangyo
collaborative design: Yoshihiko Yoshihara (collaborative design), Shuji Tada Structural Design Office (structure), Akeno Facility Resilience Inc. (equipment),
ICHIRO NISHIWAKI DESIGN OFFICE INC. (environmental design)

Art Museum & Library, Ota
location: Gunma, Japan
principal use: library, museum
scale: 3 stories, 1 basement
structure: reinforced concrete, steel frame
site area: 1,497m²
total floor space: 3,150m²
design period: 2014.4-2015.3
construction period: 2015.5-2016.12
constructor: Ishikawa kensetsu
collaborative design: ARUP (structure, equipment), Akeno Facility Resilience Inc. (disaster prevention), Izumi Okayasu (lighting), SfG (landscaping), Youko Ando design (textiles), Atsushi Hirano / AFFORDANCE (signs),
workshop collaborator: Akira Suzuki (Musashino Art University / reading advisor), Natsumi Takeda (plug in-plus / art advisor), Shigemasa Ujihara (facilitator), Tomie Kikuchi (workshop collaborator), En (Maebashi (Maebashi Institute of Technology / workshop collaborator)

Itsukushima Roof
location: unbuilt / Hiroshima, Japan
principal use: ferry terminal
scale: 2 stories
structure: steel frame, reinforced concrete
site area: 13,427m²
total floor space: 3,410m²
design period: 2016.5-2016.7
construction period: -
constructor: -
collaborative design: Mitsuhiro Kanada (structure), Masako Yamazaki / GA Yamazaki, JR West Japan Consultants Company

Akihisa HIRATA
Architect; Associate Professor at Kyoto University

1971   Born in Osaka Prefecture
1994   Graduates from the school of architecture at Kyoto University
1997   After completing a master's degree in engineering at Kyoto University,
       begins working at Toyo Ito & Associates
2005   Establishes the Akihisa Hirata Architecture Office
2015- Becomes an associate professor at Kyoto University

[Awards]
2004   The Space Design Review's Asakura Award
2008   The Japan Institute of Architects' 2007 New Face Award
2012   The Elita Design Award
2012   The Golden Lion at the 13th Venice Architecture Biennale (collaborative prize for the Japan Pavilion exhibition, Architecture. Possible here? Home-for-All)
2015   The Architectural Design Award of Nippon Prize
2018   The 31st Murano Togo Prize

[Published Works]
2009   *Animated* (A Conceptual Viewpoint), Graphic-sha
2009   *Architectural Principles for 20XX* (coauthor), INAX Publishing
2010   *The Reading Ability of Architects* (coauthor), TOTO Publishing
2011   *Contemporary Architect's Concept Series 8: Akihisa Hirata – Tangling*, LIXIL Publishing
2013   *Architecture. Possible here? Home-for-All* (coauthor), TOTO Publishing

平田晃久
建築家、京都大学准教授

1971   大阪府に生まれる
1994   京都大学工学部建築学科卒業
1997   京都大学大学院工学研究科修了後、伊東豊雄建築設計事務所勤務
2005   平田晃久建築設計事務所を設立
2015- 京都大学准教授

[受賞歴]
2004   SDレビュー2004 朝倉賞
2008   第19回JIA新人賞
2012   Elita Design Award
2012   第13回ベネチアビエンナーレ国際建築展金獅子賞（日本館協働受賞）
2015   日本建築設計学会賞
2018   第31回村野藤吾賞

[著書]
2009   『Animated（発想の視点）』グラフィック社
2009   『20XX年の建築原理へ』共著／INAX
2010   『建築家の読書術』共著／TOTO出版
2011   『現代建築家コンセプト・シリーズ8 平田晃久　建築とは〈からまりしろ〉をつくることである』LIXIL出版
2013   『ここに、建築は、可能か』共著／TOTO出版

Credit

Photographs
写真

Yasushi Ichikawa｜市川靖史：p. 010
Nacása & Partners Inc.：p. 019, pp. 060-062, pp. 124-129, pp. 150-157, p. 173 below, pp. 185-187, pp. 240-241, pp. 245-247
Kenji Nishida｜西田賢司：p. 020
Taka Ishii Gallery｜タカ・イシイギャラリー：p. 025
Yukikazu Ito｜伊藤之一：pp. 028-029
SOBAJIMA, Toshihiro / punctum｜傍島利浩：pp. 035-039, pp. 064-065, pp. 070-071, pp. 078-079, pp. 174-181, pp. 190-193, pp. 228-231, pp. 236-239
Koichi Torimura｜鳥村鋼一：pp. 046-051
Satoshi Shigeta｜繁田諭：p. 059
Daici Ano｜阿野太一：pp. 072-073, pp. 138-145, pp. 248-249, pp. 252-267
Vincent Hecht：pp. 080-081, pp. 086-093
Shinkenchiku-sha｜新建築社：pp. 094-095, p. 108, p. 135 above, p. 135 below left, p. 244, p. 251
Rebecca Emery：p. 098 left
Kazuyoshi Miyamoto｜宮本和義：p. 102
NASA, ESA, H. Teplitz (IPAC/Caltech), M. Rafelski (STScI), A. Koekemoer (STScI), R. Windhorst (Arizona State University), and Z. Levay (STScI)：p. 106
Tomohiro Sakashita｜坂下智広：p. 111
Toshiyuki Yano｜矢野紀行：pp. 112-123, pp. 130-134, p. 135 below right, pp. 136-137
Takumi Ota｜太田拓実：pp. 158-161, pp. 164-172, p. 173 above
Art Museum & Library,Ota, Shinya Kigure +Lo.cul.P：p. 194
Nezu Museum｜根津美術館：p. 200
Geospatial Information Authority of Japan｜国土地理院：p. 204
（国土地理院長の承認を得て、同院撮影の空中写真を複製したものである。（承認番号 平20関複、第166号））
Kohei Kumagai｜熊谷鋼平：p. 209
Dean Cheng：pp. 212-219
Luca Gabino：p. 278

Drawings
図版

Akihisa Hirata：p. 016, p. 024, p. 027, p. 030, p. 082, p. 103, p. 126 right, p. 250, p. 252 left
Kei Ichigo：p. 019, p. 021, p. 104 left, p. 184 below, p. 196
Kuramochi + Oguma：pp. 040-042, pp. 044-045, pp.268-269
Sayaka Matsui：p. 048, p. 056
Image courtesy by NASA：p. 104 right
Translated by Takenobu Watanabe, Bernard Rudofsky "Architecture Without Architects" (Kajima Institute Publishing Co., LTD., 1984)｜バーナード・ルドフスキー著 渡辺武信訳『建築家なしの建築』（鹿島出版会、1984）、p. 044：p. 202
Translated by Keiko Nakamura, Lynn Margulis "The Symbiotic Planet: A New Look at Evolution" (Science Masters, 1998)｜リン・マーギュリス『共生生命体の30億年』：p. 17：p. 204
Makoto Inoue：p. 242
ARUP JAPAN：p. 262 above colum center and below right

Photographs and Illustrations not listed above: Akihisa Hirata Architecture Office
上記以外の写真・図版：平田晃久建築設計事務所

English Translations
英訳

Christopher Stephens｜クリストファー・スティブンズ

Staff List

Current Staff Members

Akihisa Hirata
Yuko Tonogi
Takahito Sekiguchi
Ayami Takada
Ayaka Matsuda
Masatoshi Sugiyama
Naoki Nakamata
Minoru Aoyama
Kei Ichigo
Rei Shibuya
Masatoshi Nishizato
Eito Kitajima

Former Staff Members

Makoto Inoue
Kohei Oba
Shigetaka Nakajima
Keika Sato
Tomoki Shioya
Makiko Suda
Ayaka Matsushita
Sayaka Matsui
Hitomi Namiki
Yuji Kanno

Former Cooperating Staff Members

So Sawada
Yuuta Satake
Iria DelaPeña Mendez
Ryozo Arai

Akihisa HIRATA Discovering New
平田晃久建築作品集

2018年5月23日　初版第1刷発行
2019年9月10日　初版第2刷発行

著者：平田晃久

発行者：伊藤剛士
発行所：TOTO出版（TOTO株式会社）
〒107-0062 東京都港区南青山1-24-3 TOTO乃木坂ビル2F
[営業] TEL: 03-3402-7138 FAX: 03-3402-7187
[編集] TEL: 03-3497-1010
URL: https://jp.toto.com/publishing

デザイン：藤田裕美

印刷・製本：大日本印刷株式会社

落丁本・乱丁本はお取り替えいたします。
本書の全部又は一部に対するコピー・スキャン・デジタル化等の無断複製行為は、著作権法上での例外を除き禁じます。本書を代行業者等の第三者に依頼してスキャンやデジタル化することは、たとえ個人や家庭内での利用であっても著作権上認められておりません。
定価はカバーに表示してあります。

© 2018 Akihisa Hirata

Printed in Japan
ISBN978-4-88706-373-0